done
in a
day

Banff

→ The 10 Premier Hikes!

Where to invest your limited hiking time
to enjoy the greatest scenic reward

by KATHY + CRAIG COPELAND

hiking camping.com

Heading outdoors
eventually leads within.

The first people on earth were hikers and campers. So today, when we walk the earth and bed down on it, we're living in the most primitive, elemental way known to our species. We're returning to a way of life intrinsic to the human experience. We're shedding the burden of millennia of civilization. We're seeking catharsis. We're inviting enlightenment.

hikingcamping.com publishes unique guidebooks – literate, entertaining, opinionated – that ensure you make the most of your precious time outdoors. Our titles cover some of the world's most spectacular wild lands.

nomads@hikingcamping.com   hiking camping.com

Copyright © 2007
by Craig & Kathy Copeland
All Rights Reserved
First edition, December 2007
Updated First edition, June 2011

Published in Canada by
hikingcamping.com, inc.
P.O. Box 8563
Canmore, Alberta, T1W 2V3 Canada

readers: nomads@hikingcamping.com
retailers: orders@hikingcamping.com

All photos by the authors

Cover and interior design by www.subplot.com

Maps and production by C.J. Poznansky, giddyupgraphics@mac.com

Printed in China by Asia Pacific Offset

Library and Archives Canada Cataloguing in Publication

Copeland, Kathy, 1959-
    Banff : the 10 premier hikes / by Kathy & Craig Copeland.
(Done in a day)

Includes index.   ISBN 978-0-9783427-0-8

        1. Hiking—Alberta—Banff National Park—Guidebooks.
2. Trails—Alberta—Banff National Park—Guidebooks. 3. Banff
National Park (Alta.)--Guidebooks. I. Copeland, Craig, 1955- II. Title.
III. Series: Copeland, Kathy, 1959- Done in a day.

GV199.44.C22B36 2007   796.522097123'32   C2007-902721-0

Contents

done in a day Banff

TRIPS AT A GLANCE

The trips are listed according to difficulty, starting with the easiest and working up to the most challenging. After the trip name is the round-trip distance, followed by the elevation gain. Some trips have shorter or longer options.

1	Tunnel Mountain	4.8 km (3 mi)	240 m (787 ft)
2	Rock Isle & Grizzly lakes	7.9 km (4.9 mi)	180 m (590 ft)
3	Castle Lookout	7.4 km (4.6 mi)	520 m (1705 ft)
4	Johnston Canyon Inkpots	11.6 km (7.2 mi)	306 m (1005 ft)
	Mystic Pass	29 km (18 mi)	1001 m (3282 ft)
5	Lake Minnewanka	16.4 km (10.2 mi)	100 m (328 ft)
	Aylmer Lookout	23.4 km (14.5 mi)	662 m (2172 ft)
	Aylmer & pass	30.2 km (18.7 mi)	1026 m (3366 ft)
6	Citadel Pass	18.6 km (11.5 mi)	700 m (2296 ft)
7	Cory & Edith passes	12.9 km (8 mi)	1000 m (3280 ft)
8	Healy Pass	18.4 km (11.4 mi)	655 m (2150 ft)
9	Mt. Bourgeau	19.2 km (12 mi)	1046 m (3431 ft)
10	Cascade Mountain	21 km (13 mi)	1557 m (5108 ft)

Sunset, from Mt. Bourgeau

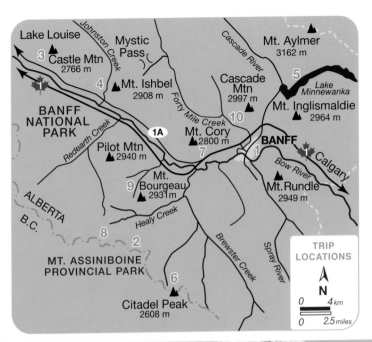

Howard Douglas Lake (Trip 6)

*Banff townsite below Cascade Mountain,
from Sulphur Mountain*

WOW

Your time is short, but the mountains are endless. So here you go: the ten Banff-area dayhikes most likely to make you say "Wow!" Plus our boot-tested opinions: why we recommend each trail, what to expect, how to enjoy the optimal experience.

We hope our suggestions compel you to get outdoors more often and stay out longer. Do it to cultivate your wild self. It will give you perspective. Do it because the backcountry teaches simplicity and self-reliance, qualities that make life more fulfilling. Do it to remind yourself why wilderness needs and deserves your protection. A bolder conservation ethic develops naturally in the mountains. And do it to escape the cacophony that muffles the quiet, pure voice within.

Where Exactly?

The town of Banff (pronounced *Bamph*) is in the lower left-hand corner of Alberta, and in the lower right-hand corner of Banff National Park.

By car, it's 850 km (528 mi) northeast of Vancouver—a long day's drive. It's 400 km (250 mi) southwest of Edmonton, via Jasper and the Icefields Parkway. And it's 128 km (80 mi) west of Calgary.

Flight times to Calgary International Airport (YYC) are 80 minutes from Vancouver (YVR), three hours from Los Angeles (LAX), and less than four hours from Chicago (ORD).

Most people reach Banff via the Trans-Canada (Hwy 1) from Calgary, where a million people live near the Bow River. Just 45-minutes beyond the city limits, the prairie abruptly ends as you pierce a wall between worlds: the Canadian Rockies.

Within an hour you'll pass Canmore—gritty coal-mining hamlet turned posh resort village. You'll glimpse it, however, only if you tear your gaze from the towering peaks that gird the Bow River Valley.

Cascade Mountain (Trip 10) soars above Banff Avenue.

Just beyond Canmore, enter Banff National Park. To see the entry-fee schedule before arriving, visit www.pc.gc.ca/pn-np/ab/banff, click on "visitor information," then click on "fees."

Fifteen minutes farther, you'll reach latitude 51° 10' 39" N, longitude 115° 34' 24" W. Welcome to Banff, highest community in Canada: elevation 1383 m (4537 ft).

Hike First, Read Later

Because our emphasis here is efficient use of limited time, we don't expect you to read the rest of this introduction.

Not immediately, anyway.

Beyond page 21 it's not necessary, unless you're a novice hiker or tentative in new territory.

We resent guidebooks that begin with a perfunctory *How To Use This Book* section. As if it were required reading. As if books were a strange, new marvel. We assume you feel the same.

If you're seasoned and confident, we figure you'll flip to the ten premier hikes, then dash onto the trail of your choice, just as we would.

Read or hike? No contest. The greatest book of all is the earth itself. Going on a hike is a way of turning the pages.

But before Banff is in your rearview mirror, keep reading. At least through page 21.

It won't take long. And what you learn will top-up your understanding of a place that's going to be on your mind a long, long time after you leave.

Cascade Mountain, from Lake Minnewanka Road

The Roaring Rockies

Imagine the earth's topography is a physical manifestation of sound. Hills would be yawns. Bigger mountains would be yells. And the peaks in the Canadian Rockies would be screams, howls, shrieks, screeches and roars.

Other ranges, blunt and cloaked in forest, are shy compared to this brazen northern breed. Here, the mountains are extroverts who bare their full, rock-hard musculature for all to see.

The cliffs are sheer and soaring. The summits sharp and serrated. And there seems no end to their spiky multitude. From a high vantage in Banff National Park, the horizon resembles a shark's mouth: row upon row of wicked incisors.

These peaks are the guardians of an immense Canadian wilderness. The heart of the range—an area larger than New Jersey—is protected by six contiguous national and provincial parks, where wolves, grizzly bears, elk, caribou, bighorn sheep, mountain goats and their alpine brethren outnumber human residents.

Together, the parks were designated a UNESCO World Heritage Site due to their "outstanding universal value," "superlative natural phenomena," and "exceptional natural beauty and aesthetic importance."

Glaciers tumble down the mountainsides. Untamed rivers careen into the valleys. You could hike into this vastness and be swallowed by it, evading human contact for weeks.

Or you could book your whole family into a luxurious castle. Go rafting, canoeing, flyfishing, horseback riding, golfing. Indulge in exotic spa treatments. Admire Inuit art. Savour French cuisine and Belgian chocolates. Sip a bottle of 1959 Chateau Haut Brion Premier Grand Cru.

You could also take your seat just a few feet from the stage in a venue little bigger than your own home and enjoy a Dave Douglas jazz concert or a Paul Taylor Dance Company performance.

That's Banff. The mountains are cold, hard and unforgiving. But the town has pastry chefs, jewelry stores, and limousines. It makes for a galvanizing summer vacation.

Only here might your après-aventure pleasures include admiring a rococo valise in the Louise Vuitton store, then glancing out the window to see a bull elk the size of a Ford pickup ambling down the street.

Après l'aventure

Between storming the summits and hitting the sack, most hikers have Homer Simpson-size appetites. And Banff has a surfeit of restaurants. Many are good. A few are superb.

Make dinner reservations at Eden, the Rimrock Hotel's five-diamond restaurant (300 Mountain Avenue, 1-888-746-7625, www.rimrockresort.com). You'll enjoy an intoxicating dining experience even if you don't order a flight of wines to accompany your six-course meal. The menu is traditional French with New World accents and Asian flair.

Seeking more for less? Head for Barpa Bill's (223 Bear Street, 762-0377). This tiny Greek cafe serves souvlaki—succulent lamb drizzled with garlic tzatziki sauce on chewy pita bread—that would inspire Zorba to break into song.

Hunger at bay, let your tour of the town commence. In Banff, gastronomy is not the only flourishing art.

Find out who's on stage at the Banff Centre (St. Julien Road, www.banffcentre.ca, 762-6100), where musicians and dancers from around the globe come to study and perform.

Check out the current exhibition at the Whyte Museum of the Canadian Rockies (111 Bear Street, 762-2291). It houses 4,000 works, both historical and contemporary, by artists who've lived in the area for at least a year, have worked here over several years, or have used the area as inspiration or subject.

You'll find more creations by elite local painters and sculptors at Canada House Gallery (201 Bear Street, 800-419-1298) and the Mountain Gallery (760-2382) in the Banff Springs Hotel.

Your kids aren't aficionados of fine art? Good. They're normal. Tell them Banff has a carnival ride: the Banff Gondola (800-760-6934). It swoops to the panoramic summit of Sulphur Mountain, where a ridgecrest boardwalk leads 0.5 km (0.3 mi) to 2270-m (7446-ft) Sanson Peak.

Beside the Bow River Bridge, the Banff Park Museum (91 Banff Avenue, 762-1558) showcases a fascinating collection of stuffed, mounted animals: more than 5,000 specimens. If foul weather keeps you and the kids indoors, you can marvel at most of Banff National Park's wildlife right here.

Of course the town's biggest museum also provides four-star accommodation. Known as "the castle in the Rockies," the Banff Springs Hotel (405 Spray Avenue, 762-2211) is indeed an enormous, brooding castle beside the Bow River, within earshot of rollicking Bow Falls.

From afar, the hotel has the enchanting appearance of standing alone in the wilderness. Within its three-foot-thick rundle-stone walls, you can wander grand hallways festooned with coats of arms, portraits of royalty, and tapestries depicting unicorns, lions and maidens.

Or you can find a hidden nook, settle into a high-backed, brocaded chair, and—refreshment in hand, novel in lap—declare yourself the temporary, benevolent monarch of your own tranquil realm while the rain that kept you from hiking patters on the leaded-glass windows.

Be sure to peruse the hotel's fascinating historical photo gallery above the reception area. And at least take a peek at the Willow Stream Spa, where the international moneyed class gets steamed, scrubbed, rubbed, soothed, wrapped, plucked, waxed, fluffed and buffed to perfection.

The centerpiece of this 38,000-square-foot monument to personal renewal is a domed sanctuary where you can soak in a series of three cascade pools of varying temperatures before floating in a therapeutic Hungarian mineral bath pulsing with hypnotic, underwater music.

Opulence, however, is just one facet of Banff, unless of course you're referring to the scenery. Sure, you can probe the limits of your platinum credit card here, but the most popular activity is free: probing the wilderness and, in the process, challenging your limits as an outdoor athlete.

For the most part, it's a town where hiking boots are welcome attire. Where wealth is not conspicuous, but prowess on the slopes and at the crags is intimidatingly so.

Chat up the locals, and you'll find they're here for the same reasons you're drawn to the ads in the real-estate office windows. Take Albert Moser, for example.

For 29 years, Albert has been the sole proprietor of an exquisite French restaurant called Le Beaujolais (212 Buffalo Street, 762-2712). Every dish on his traditional French menu would please a sophisticated Parisian.

So why is he here rather than in San Francisco or New York where his talent would earn him greater fame and fortune?

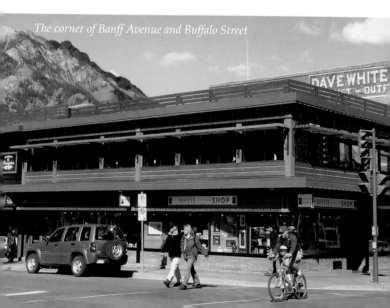

The corner of Banff Avenue and Buffalo Street

Albert loves the mountains. That's not to say he gazes lovingly at them. Albert climbs them, exuberantly, as often as he can. So do many of his staff. So do all the other mountain-mad locals.

Being with such people, if only briefly, will confirm that, yes, what you feel here in the Canadian Rockies is real. These mountains *are* speaking to you, in a soul-rousing language all their own.

A Feral Backyard

The town of Banff is on the Bow River, in a mountain sanctum of startling beauty known as the *Bow River Valley*.

The name *Bow* refers to the reeds that grew on the banks of the river. Natives used these reeds to make hunting bows. The Peigan name for the river is *Makhabn*, or *river where bow weeds grow*.

Evidence found on the shores of nearby Lake Minnewanka and Vermilion Lakes indicate human habitation 12,000 years ago.

Archaeologists believe Athabascan hunters and gatherers, tracking ice-age animals, were the first to arrive. Later, nomadic aboriginals traversed the mountains and followed the rivers east into the prairie, in search of bison.

Many Native tribes crossed paths in the Bow Valley, including the Cree, Plains Blackfeet, Stoney, Kootenai, Tsuu T'ina, Kainai, Peigan, Siksika, and Sarcee. They lived in relative peace for thousands of years.

By the mid-nineteenth century, the Stoney—who call themselves *Nakodah* and are relatives of the Assiniboine and Sioux from the east—considered these mountains their home and hunting grounds.

They settled in the region because fish and wildlife were abundant, and because frequent chinooks (strong, warm winds rushing over the mountains onto the prairie) moderated the winter climate.

done
in a
day

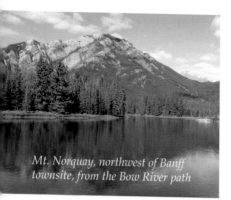

Mt. Norquay, northwest of Banff townsite, from the Bow River path

But North American aboriginal culture was shattered in the 1700s, when Europeans trickled then flooded across the continent, introducing guns, horses and new diseases.

Tribal discord increased as dramatic power shifts occurred. Territorial conflicts broke out. Violence proliferated. A smallpox epidemic annihilated 60% of the western aboriginal population. Meanwhile, the white invaders slaughtered the great buffalo herds—a critical Native food source—nearly to extinction.

The first European to approach the Canadian Rockies did so in 1754. The Palliser Expedition mapped the south end of the range in the late 1850s.

In 1883, the Canadian National Railroad laid track through the Rocky Mountains via the Bow River Valley. Three CPR workers discovered hot springs at the foot of what is now called Sulphur Mountain. They began bickering about who owned it.

At the time, the nearby settlement was known only by its railway designation: Siding 29. That changed in 1884 when it was named *Banff* by a CPR director whose birthplace was Banffshire, Scotland.

In 1885, Canada completed its transcontinental railroad linking the Atlantic and Pacific oceans and establishing a vital trade route between Europe and the Orient.

The Banff hot-springs ownership dispute was also settled that year when the Prime Minister declared it a public park. Though small—a mere 26 sq km (10 sq mi)—the reserve was Canada's first national park. The original name was *Rocky Mountains Park*. Its boundaries were soon expanded.

To stimulate westward travel, the CPR built luxurious hotels in the Rockies, starting with the Banff Springs Hotel in 1888. Its massive size, romantic fusion of Scottish baronial and French chateau styles, and wilderness setting at the confluence of the Bow and Spray Rivers endowed it with a mythic

Banff Springs Hotel

aura that was, and remains, uniquely compelling.

"If we cannot export the scenery," said the railway's visionary president, "we shall import the tourists." And they did, by carving out hiking trails, importing Swiss mountain guides to lead hotel guests onto the icefields and up the peaks, and advertising the Rockies as "50 Switzerlands in one."

They even hired British mountaineer Edward Whymper, the first to summit the Matterhorn, to climb in the Canadian Rockies then write newspaper and journal articles promoting the region.

Banff quickly became popular with wealthy European tourists, who sailed across the Atlantic on luxury liners then continued to Banff via train. Among them were kings, queens and movie stars.

Park visitation expanded beyond the aristocracy after 1911, when it became possible to drive a car from Calgary to Banff. Bus tours started in 1916.

A Winter Carnival in 1917 initiated winter tourism in Banff. Carnival events included cross-country skiing, ski jumping, curling, snowshoeing, and *skijoring* in which ski racers were hitched to dogs.

done in a day **Banff**

Banff's sole industrial enterprise, the Bankhead coal mine at the base of Cascade Mountain, operated from 1903 until 1922. Meanwhile, continued road building furthered the town's transition to a tourism-based economy.

The road from Banff to Lake Louise was completed in 1921. The first highway across the Rockies—linking Alberta and B.C. via Banff and Radium—opened in 1923. It connected routes from the U.S., creating what Americans called the "Grand Circle Tour." Today more than 90% of park visitors arrive by private vehicle.

In 1930, Rocky Mountains Park was renamed *Banff National Park*. But the boundaries continued changing until 1949, when the park's size was fixed at 6641 sq km (2564 sq mi).

Banff's downhill ski resorts—Sunshine Village and Mount Norquay—developed in the 1930s, firmly establishing the town as a winter resort.

By 1940, the Icefields Parkway pierced Banff Park's northern reaches near the Columbia Icefield and connected the towns of Banff and Jasper. This and other park infrastructure was largely built during WWI by Slavic Canadian internees, and during the Great Depression through public works projects funded by the Canadian Unemployment and Farm Relief Act.

The Trans-Canada Highway was officially opened in 1962, making Banff even more accessible to tourists. And in 1985 the town's fame was burnished by the United Nations Educational Scientific and Cultural Organization (UNESCO), who declared all of the contiguous Canadian Rocky Mountain parks a World Heritage Site.

Starting in 1976, The Banff Center organized the annual Banff Mountain Film Festival celebrating mountain culture. Festival speakers have included Reinhold Messner, Yvon Chouinard, and Sir Edmund Hillary.

When Calgary hosted the 1988 Winter Olympic Games, several events held at the Canmore Nordic Centre, a 20-minute

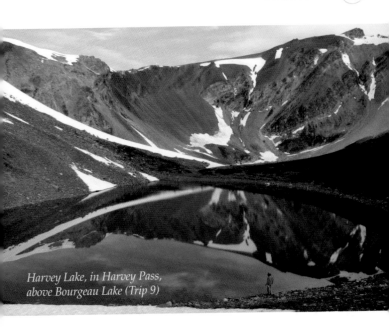

Harvey Lake, in Harvey Pass,
above Bourgeau Lake (Trip 9)

drive from Banff, just outside the park's east gate. Billions of television viewers worldwide were enamoured by the Canadian Rockies and, from then on, associated the name *Banff* with mountain splendour.

Today, nearly 4,000,000 people visit Banff National Park each year, contributing an estimated $6 billion to the economy. Almost half of them arrive in July and August.

During summer, 20% of park visitors are Europeans, 35% are from the U.S., and 42% are Canadians (23% of which are Albertans). Most come to sightsee. Some spend a few nights in the park's nearly 2,500 campsites. Only a small percentage set foot on the park's 1,600 km (1,000 mi) of hiking trails.

According to Canada's 2005 census, the town of Banff has a population of 8,352, some 7,000 of which are permanent residents. Those figures would be greater—far exceeding the reasonable limit of a national-park settlement—but Banff

Elk

passed a *need to reside* law in the 1960s. Only persons employed in the town are allowed to live there.

Elk, however, are scofflaws. Once they acquired a taste for city life—no predators, big smorgasbord (golf courses and lawns)—more than 100 of them stayed. And despite their docile, indifferent demeanor, elk are fast, easily perturbed during autumn rut, and can be dangerously aggressive. Inevitably, several people were gored, stomped, or (!) both. So Parks Canada removed the thugs en masse.

Banff remains a frontier town nonetheless. Elk still prowl Banff Avenue. Bear-proof garbage bins are still necessary. And the postcards still don't lie; the mountains are as wildly beautiful as ever.

Surrounded by the nation's flagship park, the town is symbolic of Canada's unique status in the human imagination: a modern state, with a huge, feral backyard.

Sky Jazz

Some mountains, especially volcanoes—Mt. Kilimanjaro, Mt. Fuji, Mt Rainier for example—have what appear from a distance to be relatively smooth slopes. Like the chord progression in a traditional song, they break the horizon gently, rise unbroken to a crescendo, then gradually resolve back into the horizon.

Not so the Canadian Rockies. In musical terms, these mountains are avant-garde. They've abandoned not just chord progressions,

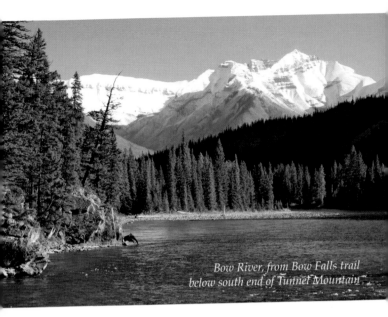

*Bow River, from Bow Falls trail
below south end of Tunnel Mountain*

but chords, scales, and rhythmic meters in favour of improvisation. The resulting shapes are fantastic. Infinitely varied. Jazz set in stone, lofted into the sky.

There were no mountains here 1.5 billion years ago. Nearby was the north shore of a vast supercontinent. Beyond were shallow, warm seas teeming with the earliest forms of multicellular life.

Between 140 million and 45 million years ago, two separate collisions of continental plates (moving slower than the speed of a growing fingernail) pushed up sedimentary rock—shale, limestone, dolomite, sandstone, quartz—from the ancient ocean floor. Thrust skyward, it formed the Canadian Rockies, which are now a middle-aged mountain range.

In Banff National Park, there are many types of mountains: complex, irregular, anticlinal, synclinal, castellate, dogtooth, and sawback. But the structure most visitors soon think of as "classically Banff" are called *dip-slope* mountains. One side is

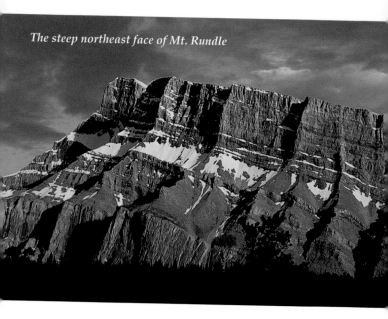

The steep northeast face of Mt. Rundle

steep, the other gradual. Mt. Rundle, looming above the southeast edge of Banff townsite, is a dip-slope massif.

Once built, mountains are immediately torn down. It's slow, tedious work. Glacial ice is the patient, demolition-crew boss. Its erosional influence is evident in the U-shape of the Bow River Valley, and in the numerous hanging valleys issuing waterfalls.

Though glaciers the world over are now mere fragments compared to their ice-age magnitude, and their power to erode has diminished, more than 1,000 of them remain in Banff National Park.

Glacial meltwater also erodes mountains, and there's a lot of it here. The Columbia Icefield, at the park's northern tip, is a hydrological apex. It feeds streams and rivers flowing into the Pacific, Atlantic and Arctic oceans.

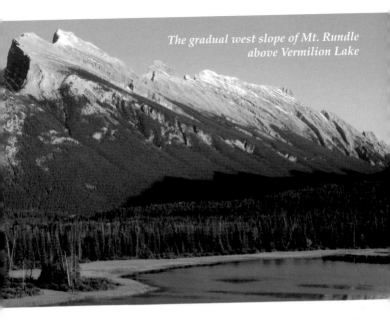

The gradual west slope of Mt. Rundle above Vermilion Lake

Before fully heeding the call of gravity, however, water tends to pool up in lakes, which in Banff Park can look surprisingly like spilled paint. You'll see every blue-green shade in the Benjamin Moore *Designer Classics* colour palette. That's because the water contains suspended rock particles (ground to dust by glaciers) that reflect sunlight.

All mountains are works in progress. But more than most, the Canadian Rockies have been immortalized in their present state by humankind's favourite art form: film.

Hollywood turned its cameras on Banff Park before moving pictures had sound. Like a burly stuntman, the range has successfully stood-in for the Swiss Alps many times.

Even the iconic, wild west that's permanently lodged between most Americans' ears is largely composed of imagery filmed in the Canadian Rockies.

Wildlife

The readily visible presence of wildlife is among the chief attractions of visiting the Canadian Rocky Mountain national parks.

Here, it's surprisingly easy to see where you stand in the food chain. Discovering you're several rungs down—by encountering a bear, for example—is both humbling and exhilarating.

It's also a healthy experience, given our species has the arrogant and harmful habit of erroneously thinking of itself as top dog.

But bears—grizzlies as well as blacks—are just one of many kinds of animals you might observe. Other creatures big and small are more frequently visible.

Watch for bats, owls, eagles (bald and golden), red-tailed hawks, osprey, falcons, woodpeckers, jays, bluebirds, Clark's nutcrackers, ptarmigan, loons, herons, and mallards.

Also be on the lookout for chipmunks, squirrels, weasels, otter, raccoons, skunks, deer, lynx, coyotes, mountain goats, bighorn sheep, caribou, and moose.

Elk frequent Banff townsite. In the evening, watch for porcupines waddling out of the forest and beavers cruising ponds. On alpine trails, you'll likely see pikas and marmots.

It's a rare and fortunate hiker who glimpses a wolf, wolverine, or cougar.

Bears

Bears are not a problem in the Canadian Rockies. But oblivious hikers often endanger themselves, other people, and the bears.

Knowledge and anticipation are all you need to hike confidently, secure in the understanding that bears pose little danger.

Only a couple hundred grizzly bears roam the Canadian Rocky Mountain national parks. The black-bear population is comparable. You're more likely to see a bear while driving the Icefields Parkway than while hiking most backcountry trails.

Grizzlies are the slowest reproducing land animals in North America. Only the musk ox is slower. So Banff Park's grizzly population will remain small.

The Banff Information Centre posts trail reports that include bear warnings and closures. Check these before your trip; adjust your plans accordingly.

Grizzlies and blacks can be difficult for an inexperienced observer to tell apart. Both species range in colour from nearly white to cinnamon to black. Full-grown grizzlies are much bigger, but a young grizzly can resemble an adult black bear, so size is not a good indicator.

The most obvious differences? Grizzlies have a dished face; a big, muscular shoulder hump; and long, curved front claws. Blacks have a straight face; no hump; and shorter, less visible front claws.

Grizzlies are potentially more dangerous than black bears, although a black bear sow with cubs can be just as aggressive. Be wary of all bears.

Any bear might attack when surprised. If you're hiking, and forest or brush limits your visibility, you can prevent surprising a bear by making noise. Bears hear about as well as humans. Most are as anxious to avoid an encounter as you are. If you warn them of your presence before they see you, they'll usually clear out.

So use the most effective noisemaker: your voice. Shout loudly. Keep it up. Don't be embarrassed. Be safe. Yell louder near streams, so your voice carries over the competing noise. Sound off more frequently when hiking into the wind. That's when bears are least able to hear or smell you coming.

To learn more, read *Bears & People* at www.pc.gc.ca/pn-np/ab/banff, or download the *Bears Beware!* MP3 at hikingcamping.com. Go to Guidebooks > Hiking > Canadian Rockies.

Grizzly bear

Bears' strongest sense is smell. They can detect an animal carcass several miles away. So don't take odourous foods on your dayhike, and never leave food scraps in your wake. Otherwise you're teaching bears to think "humans = food," furthering the possibility of a dangerous encounter.

Bears are smart. They quickly learn to associate a particular place, or people in general, with an easy meal. They become habituated and lose their fear of man. A habituated bear is a menace to any hiker within its range.

If you see a bear, don't look it in the eyes; it might think you're challenging it. Never run. Initially be still. If you must move, do it in slow motion. Bears are more likely to attack if you flee, and they're fast. A grizzly can rapidly accelerate to 50 kph (31 mph)—faster than an Olympic gold medalist sprinter. And it's a myth that bears can't run downhill.

They're also strong swimmers. Despite their ungainly appearance, they're excellent climbers too. Nevertheless, climbing a tree can be an option for escaping an aggressive bear. Some people have saved their lives this way. Others have been caught in the process.

To be out of reach of an adult bear, you must climb at least 10 m/yd very quickly, something few people are capable of. It's generally best to avoid provoking an attack by staying calm, initially standing your ground, making soothing sounds to convey a nonthreatening presence, then retreating slowly.

What should you do when a bear charges?

Black bear

If you're certain it's a lone black bear—not a sow with cubs, not a grizzly—fighting back might be effective.

If it's a grizzly, and contact seems imminent, lie face down, with your legs apart and your hands clasped behind your neck. This is safer than the fetal position, which used to be recommended, because it makes it harder for the bear to flip you over.

If you play dead, a grizzly is likely to break off the attack once it feels you're no longer a threat. Don't move until you're sure the bear has left the area, then slowly, quietly, get up and walk away. Keep moving, but don't run.

Arm yourself with pepper spray as a last defense. Keep it in a holster, on your hip belt or shoulder strap, where you can grab it fast. Many people have successfully used it to turn back charging bears.

Cayenne pepper, highly irritating to a bear's sensitive nose, is the spray's active ingredient. Without causing permanent injury, it disables the bear long enough to let you escape.

But vigilance and noise making should prevent you from ever having to spray. Do so only if you're convinced your life is at risk. You can buy pepper spray at outdoor stores. *Counter Assault* is a reputable brand.

Remember: your safety is not the only consideration. Bears themselves are at risk when confronted by people. Protecting these magnificent creatures is a responsibility hikers must accept.

Whenever bears act aggressively, they're following their natural instinct for self preservation. Often they're protecting their cubs or a food source. Yet if they maul a hiker, they're likely to be killed, or captured and moved, by wildlife management officers.

Merrily disregarding bears is foolish and unsafe. Worrying about them is miserable and unnecessary. Everyone occasionally feels afraid when venturing deep into the mountains, but knowledge and awareness can quell fear of bears.

Just take the necessary precautions and remain guardedly alert. Experiencing the grandeur of the Canadian Rockies is certainly worth risking the remote possibility of a bear encounter.

Cougars

You'll probably never see a cougar. But they live in the Canadian Rockies, and they can be dangerous, so you should know a bit about them.

Elsewhere referred to as a puma, mountain lion, or panther, the cougar is an enormous, graceful cat. An adult male can reach the size of a big human: 80 kg (175 lb), and 2.4 m (8 ft) long including a 1-m (3-ft) tail. In the Canadian Rockies, they tend to be a tawny grey.

Nocturnal, secretive, solitary creatures, cougars come together only to mate. Each cat establishes a territory of 200 to 280 sq km (125 to 175 sq mi). They favour dense forest that provides cover while hunting. They also hide among rock outcroppings and in steep canyons.

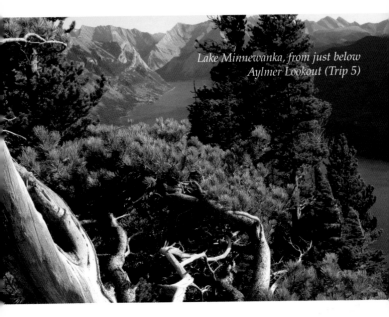

Lake Minnewanka, from just below
Aylmer Lookout (Trip 5)

Habitat loss and aggressive predator-control programs have severely limited the range of this mysterious animal that once lived throughout North America. Still, cougars are not considered endangered or threatened. Cougars appear to be thriving in western Canada.

Cougars are carnivores. They eat everything from mice to elk but prefer deer. They occasionally stalk people but rarely attack them. In folklore, cougars are called *ghost cats* or *ghost walkers*, for good reason. They're very shy and typically avoid human contact. Nevertheless, cougars have attacked solo hikers and lone cross-country skiers in the Canadian Rockies.

Cougar sightings and encounters are increasing due to a thriving cougar population, humanity's ever-expanding footprint, and the growing number of people visiting the wilderness.

If you're lucky enough to see a cougar, treasure the experience. Just remember they're unpredictable. Follow these suggestions:

- Never hike alone in areas of known cougar sightings. Keep children close to you; pick them up if you see fresh cougar scat or tracks.

- Never approach a cougar, especially a feeding one. Never flee from a cougar, or even turn your back on it. Sudden movement might trigger an instinctive attack. Avert your gaze and speak to it in a calm, soothing voice. Hold your ground or back away slowly. Always give the animal a way out.

- If a cougar approaches, spread your arms, open your jacket, do anything you can to enlarge your image. If it acts aggressively, wave your arms, shout, throw rocks or sticks. If attacked, fight back. Don't play dead.

Maps

The Gem Trek maps *Banff Up-Close* (1:35 000) and *Banff & Mt. Assiniboine* (1:100 000) were our primary references while writing this book. For hiking in the Canadian Rockies, Gem Trek topographic maps (maps@gemtrek.com) are the most helpful.

The maps we created and that accompany each trip in this book are for general orientation only. Our *On Foot* directions are elaborate and precise, so referring to a topo map shouldn't be necessary. Nevertheless, you might want one.

After reaching a summit, a topo map will enable you to interpret the surrounding geography. If the terrain through which you're hiking intrigues you, a topo map can contribute to a more fulfilling experience.

The stats box for each trip indicates which Gem Trek map to bring. You can purchase them via mail-order from Map Town in Calgary (www.maptown.com, 877-921-6277). They're also available at outdoor shops and bookstores in and near the Canadian Rockies.

Carry a Compass

Left and *right* are relative. Any hiking guidebook relying solely on these inadequate and potentially misleading terms should be shredded and dropped into a recycling bin.

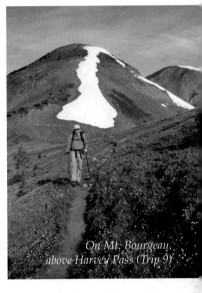

You'll find all the *On Foot* descriptions in this book include frequent compass directions. That's the simplest way to accurately, reliably guide a hiker.

What about GPS? It might be invaluable if you're trekking cross-country (off trail) long distance. But most hikers generally find a map and compass totally adequate for navigation. Following our detailed directions while hiking the trails in this book, you shouldn't need a GPS unit.

On Mt. Bourgeau, above Harvey Pass (Trip 9)

Keep in mind that the compass directions provided in this book are of use only if you're carrying a compass. Granted, our route descriptions are so detailed, you'll rarely have to check your compass. But bring one anyway, just in case.

A compass is required hiking equipment—anytime, anywhere, regardless of your level of experience, or your familiarity with the terrain.

Clip your compass to the shoulder strap of your pack, so you can glance at it quickly and easily. Even if you never have to rely on your compass, occasionally checking it will strengthen your sense of direction—an enjoyable, helpful, and conceivably lifesaving asset.

Keep in mind that our stated compass directions are always in reference to true north. In the Canadian Rockies, that's approximately 16° left of (counterclockwise from) magnetic north. If that puzzles you, read your compass owner's manual.

Physical Capability

Until you gain experience judging your physical capability and that of your companions, these guidelines might be helpful. Anything longer than an 11-km (7-mi) round-trip dayhike can be very taxing for someone who doesn't hike regularly. A 425-m (1400-ft) elevation gain in that distance is challenging but possible for anyone in average physical condition. Very fit hikers are comfortable hiking 24 km (15 mi) and ascending 1000 m (3280 ft)—or more—in a single day.

Less common, yellow paintbrush

Wilderness Ethics

We hope you're already conscientious about respecting nature and other people. If not, here's how to pay off some of your karmic debt load.

Let wildflowers live. They blossom for only a few fleeting weeks. Uprooting them doesn't enhance your enjoyment, and it prevents others from seeing them at all. We once heard parents urge a string of children to pick as many different-coloured flowers as they could find. Great. Teach kids to entertain themselves by destroying nature, so the world continues marching toward environmental collapse.

Stay on the trail. Shortcutting causes erosion. It doesn't save time on steep ascents, because you'll soon be slowing to catch your breath. On a steep descent, it increases the likelihood of injury. If hiking in a group across trail-less terrain, soften your impact by spreading out.

Roam meadows with your eyes, not your boots. Again, stay on the trail. If it's braided, follow the main path. When you're compelled to take a photo among wildflowers, try to walk on rocks.

Leave no trace. Be aware of your impact. Travel lightly on the land. After a rest stop, take a few minutes to look for and obscure any evidence of your stay. Restore the area to its natural state.

Pack out everything you bring. Never leave a scrap of trash anywhere. This includes toilet paper, nut shells, and cigarette butts. Fruit peels are also trash. They take years to decompose, and wild animals won't eat them. And don't just pack out *your* trash. Leave nothing behind, whether you brought it or not. Keep a small plastic bag handy, so picking up trash is easy.

Poop without impact. In the wilds, choose a site at least 60 m (66 yd) from trails and water sources. Ground that receives sunlight part of the day is best. Use a trowel to dig a small cat hole—10 to 20 cm (4 to 8 inches) deep, 10 to 15 cm (4 to 6 inches) wide—in soft, dark, biologically active soil. Afterward, throw a handful of dirt into the hole, stir with a stick to speed decomposition, replace your diggings, then camouflage the site. Pack out used toilet paper in a plastic bag. Always clean your hands with a moisturizing hand sanitizer, like Purell. Sold in drugstores, it comes in conveniently small, lightweight, plastic bottles.

Urinate off trail, well away from water sources. The salt in urine attracts animals. They'll defoliate urine-soaked vegetation, so aim for dirt or pine needles.

Respect the reverie of other hikers. On busy trails, don't feel it's necessary to communicate with everyone you pass. Most of us are seeking solitude, not a soiree. A simple greeting is sufficient to convey good will. Obviously, only you can judge what's appropriate at the time. But it's usually presumptuous and annoying to blurt out advice without being asked. "Boy, have you got a long way to go." "The views are much better up there." "Be careful, it gets rougher." If anyone wants to know, they'll ask. Some people are sly. They start by asking where you're going, so they can tell you all about it. Offer unsolicited information only to warn other hikers about conditions ahead that could seriously affect their trip.

Hiking With Your Dog

"Can I bring Max, my Pomeranian?"

Yes. Banff National Park allow dogs in the backcountry with the stipulation that they be leashed the entire time.

Bringing your dog hiking with you, however, isn't simply a matter of "Can I or can't I?" The larger question is "Should I or shouldn't I?"

Consider the social consequences. Most dog owners think their pets are angelic. But other hikers rarely agree.

A curious dog, even if friendly, can be a nuisance. A barking dog is annoying. A person continually yelling unheeded commands at a disobedient dog is infuriating, because it amounts to *two* annoying animals, not just one. An untrained dog, despite the owner's hearty reassurance that "he won't hurt you," can be frightening.

Consider your environmental responsibilities. Many dog owners blithely allow their pets to pollute streams and lakes. The fact that their dog is crapping in the trail doesn't occur to them, but it certainly does to the next hiker who comes along and steps in it.

Photo by Tim Rhodes

Consider the safety issues. Dogs in the backcountry are a danger to themselves. For example, they could be spiked by porcupines. Even worse, they can endanger their owners and other hikers, because dogs infuriate bears. If a dog runs off, it might reel a bear back with it.

This isn't a warning not to bring your dog. We've completed lengthy trips with friends whose dogs we enjoyed immensely. This is a plea to see your dog objectively, from the perspective of your fellow hikers.

Weather

The volatile Canadian Rocky Mountain climate will have you building shrines to placate the weather gods. Conditions change quickly and dramatically. Summer is pitifully short.

Most trails aren't snow-free until mid-June. Alpine passes can be blanketed in white until mid-July. Snowfall is possible on any day, and likely at higher elevations after August. Above treeline, the annual average temperature is below freezing, and most precipitation is snow.

The Banff Information Centre posts weather forecasts and trail-condition reports. Recorded weather forecasts are available by phone: (403) 762-2088. When the snowpack is melting in late spring and early summer, just one week of clear, sunny weather can greatly increase trail accessibility.

Regardless of the forecast, always be prepared for heavy rain, harsh winds, plummeting temperatures, sleet, hail... the whole miserable gamut. Also allow for the possibility of scorching sun and soaring temperatures. The weather can change drastically, with alarming speed. Though the sky is clear at dawn, it might be boiling with ominous black clouds by afternoon. Storms can dissipate equally fast.

Statistics indicate that, throughout the Canadian Rockies, you can expect rainfall one of every three days in summer. Even many rain-free days are cloudy. So don't squander a blue sky. Celebrate it: hike fast and far.

Charts showing Banff Park's average monthly precipitation during hiking season are of little help. June is likely to be wettest, October driest. The figures for July, August and September are too close for anyone to reliably recommend when your hiking trip is least likely to be rained out. Locals, however, will tell you that we usually get a snowstorm in early September, followed by a couple weeks of clear skies, pleasantly cool daytime temperatures, and nighttime lows around freezing.

Charts showing the average monthly maximum and minimum temperatures in the mountain parks reveal the following. By May the highs reach about 16°C (61°F), the lows stay just above freezing. In June, the highs and lows are roughly 4°C (7°F) warmer than in May. July is usually the hottest month, with highs around 24°C (75°F), lows averaging 7°C (45°F). August can be almost as hot as July, but generally isn't. September

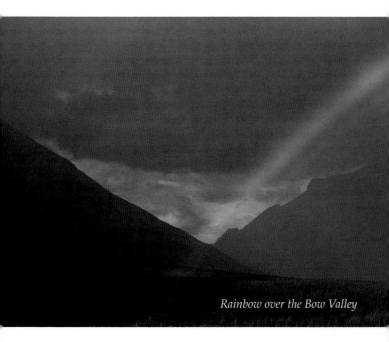

Rainbow over the Bow Valley

tends to be slightly warmer than May. In October, the highs top out near 12°C (54°F), the lows drop just below freezing.

Fall is touted by many as the ideal time to hike in the Canadian Rockies. Bugs are absent, crowds diminish, the larch trees are golden. But by then the sun is rising later and setting earlier, which restricts dayhiking. We prefer the long days of mid-summer.

Typically, the Canadian Rocky Mountain climate will grant you about two-and-a-half months of optimal high-country hiking. That's only 20% of the year. At the end of June, however, you'll have 16½ hours between sunrise (5:30 a.m.) and sunset (10 p.m.).

Carpe diem.

Lightning

Many of the trails in this book lead to meadows and ridges where, during a storm, you could be exposed to lightning.

Storms tend to develop in the afternoon, so you can try to reach alpine destinations early in the day. But it's impossible to always evade violent weather. You hike to commune with nature, the power of which can threaten your safety.

Even if you start under a cloudless, blue sky, you might see ominous, black thunderheads marching toward you a few hours later. Upon reaching a high, airy vantage, you could be forced by an approaching storm to decide if and when you should retreat to safer ground.

The following is a summary of lightning precautions recommended by experts. These are not guaranteed solutions. We offer them merely as suggestions to help you make wise choices and reduce your chance of injury.

If your hair is standing on end, there's electricity in the air around you. A lightning strike could be imminent. Get outa there! That's usually down the mountain, but if there's too much open expanse to traverse, look for closer protection.

A direct lightning strike can kill you. It can cause brain damage, heart failure or third-degree burns. Ground current, from a nearby strike, can severely injure you, causing deep burns and tissue damage. Direct strikes are worse, but ground-current contact is far more common.

Avoid a direct strike by getting off exposed ridges and peaks. Even a few meters (yards) off a ridge is better than on top. Avoid isolated, tall trees. A clump of small trees or an opening in the trees is safer.

Avoid ground current by getting out of stream gullies and away from crevices, lichen patches, or wet, solid-rock surfaces. Loose rock, like talus, is safer.

Look for a low-risk area, near a highpoint at least 10 m/yd higher than you. Crouch near its base, at least 1.5 m/yd from cliffs or walls.

Once you choose a place to wait it out, your goal is to prevent brain or heart damage by stopping an electrical charge from flowing through your whole body. Squat with your boots touching one another. If you have a sleeping pad, put it beneath your boots for insulation. Keep your hands away from rocks. Fold your arms across your chest. Stay at least 10 m/yd from your companions, so if one is hit, another can give cardiopulmonary resuscitation.

Deep caves offer protection. Crouch away from the mouth, at least 1.5 m/yd from the walls. But avoid rock overhangs and shallow depressions, because ground current can jump across them. Lacking a deep cave, you're safer in the low-risk area below a highpoint.

Hypothermia

Many deaths outdoors involve no obvious injury. "Exposure" is usually cited as the killer, but that's a misleading term. It vaguely refers to conditions related to the hikers' demise.

The actual cause is hypothermia: excessive loss of body heat. It can happen with startling speed, in surprisingly mild weather—often between 0 and 10°C (30 and 50°F).

Guard against it vigilantly.

Cool temperatures, moisture (perspiration or rain), wind, or fatigue, usually a combination, sap the body of vital warmth. Hypothermia results when heat loss continues to exceed heat gain.

Initial symptoms include chills and shivering. Poor coordination, slurred speech, sluggish thinking, and memory loss are next.

Intense shivering then decreases while muscular rigidity increases, accompanied by irrationality, incoherence, even hallucinations. Stupor, blue skin, slowed pulse and respiration, and unconsciousness follow. The heartbeat finally becomes erratic until the victim dies.

Avoid becoming hypothermic by wearing synthetic clothing that wicks moisture away from your skin and insulates when wet. Read *Prepare For Your Hike*, in the back of this book, for a description of clothing and equipment that will help you stay warm and dry.

Food fuels your internal fire, so bring more than you think you'll need, including several energy bars for emergencies only.

If you can't stay warm and dry, you must escape the wind and rain. Turn back. Keep moving. Eat snacks. Seek shelter. Do it while you're still mentally and physically capable.

Watch others in your party for signs of hypothermia. Victims might resist help at first. Trust the symptoms, not the person. Be insistent. Act immediately.

Create the best possible shelter for the victim. Take off his wet clothes and replace them with dry ones. Insulate him from the ground. Provide warmth. Build a fire. Keep the victim conscious. Feed him sweets. Carbohydrates quickly convert to heat and energy. In advanced cases, victims should not drink hot liquids.

Bighorn sheep

Larkspur

Plumed aven

Arnica

Prairie crocus

Calypso orchid

Elephant's head

done
in a
day

the hikes

Approaching the false summit (right), en route to the 2998-m (9836-ft)
true summit (left) of Cascade Mountain (Trip 10)

trip 1
⨂ tunnel mountain

location	east edge of Banff townsite
round trip	4.8 km (3 mi)
elevation gain	240 m (787 ft)
key elevations	trailhead 1450 m (4756 ft)
	summit 1690 m (5543 ft)
hiking time	1½ hours
difficulty	easy
available	April through November
map	Gem Trek *Banff Up-Close*

opinion

Purists look down their noses at Banff townsite as if it were a cancerous growth. It *is* too big, crowded and commercial, considering it's in a national park. But Banff still has charm. The setting is exquisite. Looking down your nose at it from the nearby summit of Tunnel Mtn is a fun, easy way to appreciate it.

The trailhead is less than a kilometer from the Banff Avenue tourist carnival. So you don't even need a car to escape the hubbub. No wonder the trail is so heavily used. Your best shot at solitude is, of course, evening or early morning.

You're not a hiker? Not a problem. Tunnel is more of a hill than a mountain, so the summit is an attainable goal for most people. Just don't try it in sandals or dress shoes. At least wear tennis shoes or runners. And though civilization is close, don't leave your brain behind. Carry water (there's none on the trail) and anything else you think you'll need.

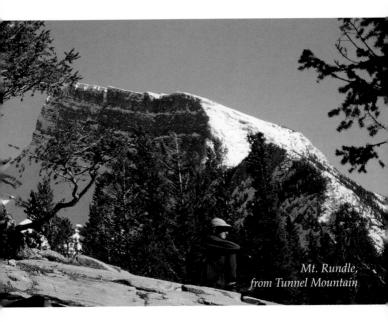

Mt. Rundle,
from Tunnel Mountain

You might wonder where the tunnel is. Well, the mountain got its name when Major A.B. Rogers, who originally routed the Canadian Pacific Railroad through Banff, inexplicably decided it should go directly beneath the mountain. But sanity prevailed. The tunnel was never blasted. The CPR simply laid their track on the north side of the valley. Nobody bothered changing the then meaningless name back to its native appellation: Sleeping Buffalo Mtn.

fact

by vehicle

From the intersection of Banff Avenue and Wolf Street (St. Paul's church is on the southeast corner), follow Wolf Street 0.5 km (0.3 mi) east to where it T's at the foot of Tunnel Mtn. Turn right on St. Julien Road, immediately bear left, and drive 0.4 km (0.25 mi) to the signed trailhead parking area on the left, at 1450 m (4756 ft).

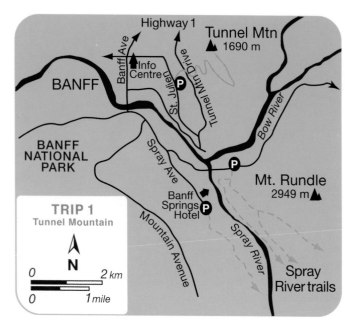

Highway 1　Tunnel Mtn
▲ 1690 m

Banff Ave

Info Centre

St. Julien

Tunnel Mtn Drive

P

BANFF

Bow River

BANFF NATIONAL PARK

Spray Ave

Banff Springs Hotel

P

Mt. Rundle
2949 m ▲

P

Mountain Avenue

Spray River

Spray River trails

TRIP 1
Tunnel Mountain

N

0 ——— 2 km
0 ——— 1 mile

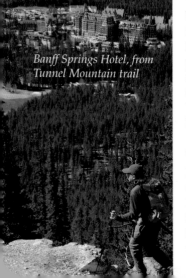

Banff Springs Hotel, from Tunnel Mountain trail

To shorten the round-trip hike by 0.6 km (0.4 mi), keep driving through the Banff Centre. Turn left onto Tunnel Mtn Drive and proceed uphill. Park in the pull-out on your left, above the Banff Centre, at 2.5 km (1.5 mi). The Tunnel Mtn trail, which started below, crosses the road here.

on foot

From the lower trailhead, ascend the forested west slope of Tunnel Mtn. Cross Tunnel Mtn Drive at 0.3 (0.2 mi). The wide trail switchbacks up through open forest on the west side of the mountain.

Near 2.2 km (1.3 mi) crest the **ridge**. Take a cautious look right (east) over the cliff. The Bow River is below. Mt. Rundle is south-east. Turn left (north) and resume the now gradual ascent.

At 2.4 km (1.5 mi), 1690 m (5543 ft), reach the **summit**: an open, rocky bluff. Looking west, you can see the Vermilion Lakes and the Massive Range. Banff townsite is 307 m (1007 ft) below. Cascade Mountain is directly north, Sulphur Mtn is south-southwest.

The east side of Tunnel Mountain, with Cascade Mountain directly north

trip 2

rock isle, grizzly and larix lakes

location	immediately south of Sunshine Ski Area
circuit	7.9 km (4.9 mi) to 11.8 km (7.3 mi)
elevation gain	180 m (590 ft) to 300 m (984 ft)
key elevations	trailhead 2195 m (7200 ft)
	Grizzly Lake 2225 m (7300 ft)
	Standish viewpoint 2420 m (7938 ft)
hiking time	3 to 4 hours
difficulty	easy
available	July through September
map	Gem Trek *Banff and Mt. Assiniboine*

opinion

Meadow cultists throng these lakes. Rock Isle averages 60 visitors on a sunny, summer day, and has hosted 130. That explains the assiduously maintained trail and the huge viewing platform that softens human impact. It also justifies the criticism that this trip is too crowded and tame to be rated *Premier*.

But ease and convenience, combined with the vast, incredible beauty of nearby Sunshine Meadows, make it a very rewarding walk for anyone unable to climb high or trek far. This is their opportunity to ingest the distilled essence of the Canadian Rockies—the opiate for which some of us continually venture deep into the lonely wilds.

The lakes themselves are lovely, but it's the meadowy, mountainous expanse fanning out in all directions that will rapidly fill your camera's memory card. On a clear day, you'll see Mt. Assiniboine thrusting its horn skyward. In fall, stands of larch trees add brilliant gold to the alpine palette, especially around Grizzly and Larix lakes.

*Rock Isle (left) and Larix (right) lakes
beneath Quartz Hill, from Standish Lookout*

Our route description begins in Sunshine Village, at 2195 m (7200 ft). To get there, you must hike the restricted-use access road or ride the White Mountain Adventures shuttle bus, both of which depart the Sunshine Ski Area gondola station.

The road ascends 520 m (1706 ft) in 6.5 km (4 mi). Walking it is a bore and a chore. We know. We've done it. You'll see nothing but unremarkable trees for 1½ hours. And you'll have to plod back down as well. Ride the shuttle. The time and effort you'll save is well worth the cost.

fact

before your trip

Visit www.sunshinemeadowsbanff.com to check the current schedule and prices for the shuttle bus operated by White Mountain Adventures (www.whitemountainadventures.com) that runs between the Sunshine Ski Area parking lot and Sunshine Village. The ticket office (403-762-7889) is open June through September.

by vehicle

Drive the Trans-Canada Hwy east 21 km (13 mi) from Castle Junction, or west 9 km (5.6 mi) from Banff townsite. Turn south onto the signed Sunshine Village road. Proceed 8.3 km (5.1 mi) to the parking lot near the gondola station, at 1675 m (5495 ft). The gondola does not operate in summer.

by bus

In the past, the first bus (mid-June through August only, advance purchase required) has departed at 8 a.m. Starting at 9 a.m. (mid-June through September, no reservations necessary) buses have departed approximately every hour, with the last bus up at 4:45 p.m. Return times have also been approximately every hour, with the last bus down at 5:30 p.m.

on foot

From Sunshine Village ski lodge, at 2195 m (7200 ft), walk south past the left (east) side of the saloon. Go uphill 200 m (220 yd) to the Parks Canada cabin. Fifteen meters past it, turn left (east-southeast) onto the well-groomed gravel path. It ascends gently. Go right (south) at the first junction, at 2290 m (7510 ft), and continue the easy ascent.

Sunshine Meadows residents

In another 5-7 minutes, reach the next junction at 1.2 km (0.7 mi). This is the **summit of the Great Divide**, at 2300 m (7544 ft). The narrower path left (south-east) leads to Citadel Pass. Go right (west) on the wider path for Rock Isle, Grizzly and Larix lakes.

Reach **Rock Isle Lake overlook** at 1.6 km (1 mi). Mt. Assiniboine is visible southeast, beyond Quartz Hill. About 200 m (220 yd) past the overlook, the **Twin Cairns trail** bears right. Stay left for Grizzly and Larix lakes. Descend to Rock Isle Lake's outlet stream. Grizzly and Larix lakes are visible below.

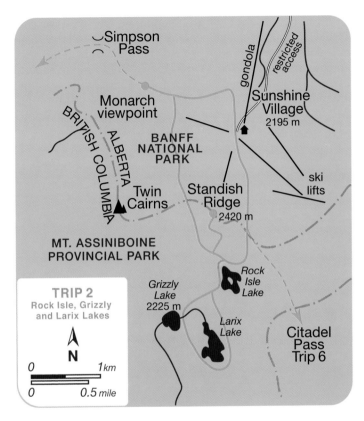

Larix, to the south, is the largest of the three. The botanical name for the alpine larch trees you see here is also Larix.

Continuing, the trail descends. Reach a **fork** at 2.7 km (1.7 mi). Go either way and loop back to this point. Keeping right, you'll drop to cross **Grizzly Lake's inlet stream** at 2225 m (7300 ft). A little farther is a viewpoint of Simpson River valley. The trail then curves back and ascends, rounding the shore of **Larix Lake** and rejoining the trail where you previously dropped to Grizzly Lake. Bear right to the familiar junction at 6.1 km (3.8 mi). Here, right leads back to Sunshine Village for a total of 7.9 km (4.9 mi).

Or, from the 6.1-km (3.8-mi) junction, go left (west) on the **Twin Cairns trail** for a longer return to Sunshine Village. Total mileage this way will be 11.8 km (7.3 mi). Go right at the next junction to ascend 120 m (395 ft) in 0.6 km (0.4 mi) to superb 2420-m (7938-ft) **Standish Viewpoint**. Descend back to the junction. Go right (northwest) for 2.3 km (1.4 mi) through meadows and subalpine forest, descending to another junction. Go right to reach Sunshine Village in 1.1 km (1.1 mi).

Rock Isle Lake

castle lookout

location	northwest of Castle Junction
round trip	7.4 km (4.6 mi)
elevation gain	520 m (1705 ft)
key elevations	trailhead 1460 m (4790 ft)
	lookout 1980 m (6495 ft)
hiking time	3 to 3½ hours
difficulty	easy
available	May through October
map	Gem Trek *Banff and Mt. Assiniboine*

opinion

As mountain wildflowers go, the prairie crocus is huge. It's eager, too, bursting out of the earth long before other spring posies have awakened in the Canadian Rockies. Though ambitious, it's not conservative. It has flamboyant lavender petals surrounding a yellow pompon of anthers. Also known as a pasque flower, it grows on dry slopes pummeled by sunshine. A prairie crocus promises snow-free hiking. And by May you'll find these beautiful harbingers of spring lining the trail to Castle Lookout— one of Banff Park's earliest available hiking destinations.

The lookout, constructed in the 1940s and abandoned in the 70s, is now gone. But the panorama it afforded—up and down the Bow Valley, and through Vermilion Pass into Kootenay Park—is as splendid as ever, well worth the steep ascent. Views begin about half an hour from the trailhead. You'll see a western horizon crowded with peaks that are especially showy when the high-elevation snowpack remains deep. You'll also see Castle Mountain's towering, astonishingly complex ramparts at close range.

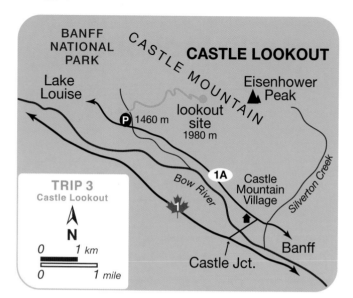

Ascending the castle's southwest flank, you'll begin on an uninspiring old road. It doesn't narrow to a trail until you're more than halfway up. Another drawback to this hike is that Hwy 1A, the Canadian National Railway, and the Trans-Canada Hwy all graze the castle premises, so dissonant metal and rubber compete with the sounds of nature, and the sight of these broad, arterial scars degrade the scenery. But when you're storming the bastille in mid-April, you'll be smiling nevertheless.

fact

by vehicle

From Lake Louise Village, drive Hwy 1A (Bow Valley Parkway) southeast 20 km (12.4 mi). From Castle Mountain Village, drive Hwy 1A northwest 5 km (3 mi). From either approach, turn north into the parking lot, at 1460 m (4790 ft).

on foot

Follow the old road departing the north end of the parking lot, right of the info kiosk. Begin a steady, moderate ascent through

Castle Mountain, above lookout trail

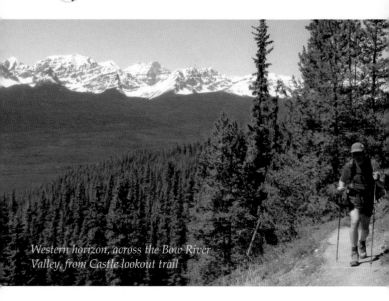

Western horizon, across the Bow River Valley, from Castle lookout trail

a forest of pine and spruce. Overall, your general direction of travel will remain east. At 1645 m (5396 ft), about 15 minutes up, pass the remains of a cabin.

The road narrows to trail at 2 km (1.2 mi), 1748 m (5733 ft)—about 30 minutes up for strong striders. A couple minutes farther, attain the first view across the Bow Valley. Left (south-southwest) is Storm Mtn. The peaks of Kootenay National Park are southwest, beyond Vermilion Pass. Glacier-hatted Mt. Temple is west-northwest.

Traverse open slopes, then switchback upward among rock outcroppings. At 1915 m (6280 ft) cross a creeklet in a steep, narrow gorge beneath Castle Mountain's fantastic turrets. After hiking 3.7 km (2.3 mi) in about an hour, arrive at the 1980-m (6495-ft) perch where the Castle Mountain Lookout once stood. The remaining cement foundation now serves as a bench. The panorama extends east-southeast to Mt. Ishbel, in the Sawback Range, and southeast to the Sundance Range, near Banff townsite.

trip 4
johnston canyon/ inkpots/mystic pass

location	southeast of Castle Junction
round trip	5.4 km (3.4 mi) to upper falls
	11.6 km (7.2 mi) to Inkpots
	29 km (18 mi) to pass
elevation gain	120 m (394 ft) to upper falls
	306 m (1005 ft) to Inkpots
	1001 m (3282 ft) to pass
key elevations	trailhead 1430 m (4690 ft)
	Inkpots 1645 m (5395 ft)
	pass 2280 m (7478 ft)
hiking time	1½ hours for canyon, 3 hours for Inkpots
	8 to 9 hours for pass
difficulty	very easy to upper falls, easy to Inkpots
	challenging to pass (due to distance)
available	May through mid-November for canyon
	June through October for Inkpots
	July through September for pass
map	Gem Trek *Banff and Mt. Assiniboine*

opinion

Toponymy is the study of place-names (toponyms), their origins, meanings, and use. It's a branch of *onomastics*, the study of all kinds of names.

And what a name: *Mystic Pass*.

Toponymy reveals that William Twin, a Stoney Indian, guided the first white people to the pass in 1891: Bill and Jim Brewster, ages 11 and 9.

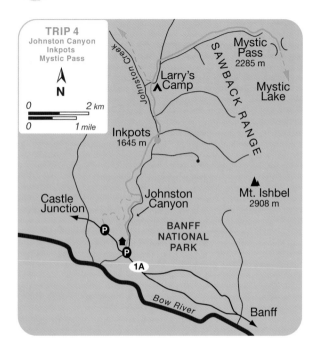

The brothers later started a tourist transportation dynasty that still thrives today. You'll see the name *Brewster* on buses throughout the Canadian Rockies.

Did the Brewster boys label the pass? If so, it was precocious of them.

But there's another way—unscientific, but equally meaningful—to account for the name. Simply study the trail leading to it. You'll find it models the spiritual path that all mystics have followed.

It's long, challenging, initially crowded, at times monotonous. Solitude awaits those who press on. Fleeting moments of revelation are followed by continued struggle. But the ultimate destination is sublime.

Specifically, the journey begins in Johnston Canyon, which is flooded every summer with windshield tourists. They're here

Inkpots and Mt. Ishbel, Johnston Creek Valley

Lower Johnston Canyon

because the chasms and cascades are fantastic, and because the paved, mostly-level path accommodates waddlers and toddlers.

So despite the Disneyesque atmosphere, it's worth seeing. But do not follow the crowd, which largely turns around at the canyon's upper falls. Where they retreat, carry on. A brief ascent will allow you a peek at the upper canyon before you drop into Johnston Creek Valley.

You'll soon arrive at the Inkpots, where cold springs bubbling to the earth's surface have formed serenely beautiful, aquamarine pools. Look up, and you'll see picturesque Mt. Ishbel, one of the many peaks comprising the Sawback Range.

Still, you won't be alone here. And though the Inkpots' setting is pleasant, it doesn't compare to the beauty of the trip's climax. So polish off that Power Bar and press on.

In midsummer, when the sun doesn't set until 10 p.m., fleet, zealous hikers who start early can tag the pass and return to Banff by suppertime. And it's worth the effort.

For motivation, look again at the photo on the cover of this book. See how many other hikers are there? That's another reward you'll likely enjoy at Mystic Pass: solitude.

Plus, you'll earn a lasting sense of accomplishment for having deeply probed the Canadian Rockies—a feat few visitors even attempt.

Mystic Lake

And here's one final enticement. After reaching the pass, if you can marshal another burst of steam, the crest of the Sawback Range beckons. It affords an aerial view of the pass, the surrounding mountains, Forty Mile Creek Valley, and the Vermilion Range.

fact

by vehicle

Drive Highway 1A (Bow Valley Parkway) to Johnston Canyon. It's 6.5 km (4 mi) southeast of Castle Village (across the Bow River from Castle Junction), or 17.5 km (10.9 mi) northwest of the Trans-Canada junction near Banff townsite. Parking is on the northeast side of the highway, on both sides of the creek, at 1430 m (4690 ft).

on foot

Cross the bridge over Johnston Creek to the resort side, turn right, and follow the path upstream (generally north) above the left (west) bank.

The catwalks in Johnston Canyon are 1.6 km (1 mile) long.

Ascending the narrow canyon, you'll cross steel-and-concrete catwalks attached to rock walls. Reach the **lower falls** at 1.1 km (0.7 mi).

Pass two cascades at 1.8 km (1.1 mi). Paved path continues to the 30-m (100-ft) **upper falls** at 2.7 km (1.7 mi), 1550 m (5084 ft).

Beyond the falls, the trail climbs to merge with an old road from Moose Meadows at 3.2 km (2 mi), 1602 m (5255 ft). Stay right at this junction. A moderate ascent through forest tops out at 1736 m (5695 ft).

While descending north-northeast, attain glimpses into upper Johnston Canyon. The grade steepens into Johnston Creek Valley, where the view expands.

At 5.8 km (3.6 mi), 1645 m (5396 ft), about 1½ hours from the trailhead, arrive at the **Inkpots**—small, round pools of aquamarine water, formed by mineral springs.

Trivia Alert: The Inkpots maintain a constant temperature of 4° C (39.2° F). What you see at the bottom of the pools is quicksand.

The pools are just above Johnston Creek. Surrounding them is a meadow full of willows and dwarf birch. Several benches invite you to rest and appreciate the journey's first significant vista. The dominate sight is southeast: 2850-m (9348-ft) Mt. Ishbel.

Bound for Mystic Pass? The trail stays left (northwest) of the Inkpots, heading up-valley (north-northeast). In two minutes, cross a large, wood bridge over **Johnston Creek**. On the east bank, the trail turns left (north).

Hop over braided meltwater streams. After a short, steep ascent, the trail levels in forest again. Reach **Larry's Camp** at 7.9 km (4.9 mi), 1677 m (5500 ft).

Immediately beyond, the trail drops to an unnamed tributary of Johnston Creek. Go right (east) upstream, cross the creek on a bridge, and arrive at a signed junction on the tributary's north bank.

The Johnston Creek Valley trail proceeds straight (northwest), eventually crossing Pulsatilla Pass. For Mystic Pass, go right (northeast), following the tributary upstream.

In ten minutes, cross a bridge to the east bank. You're in deep forest now. About 15 minutes of moderate ascent is followed by a ten-minute level respite.

Lower Johnston Falls

At 1838 m (6030 ft), about 30 minutes above the junction, cross a creek on awkward logs and continue ascending northeast. Soon reach a grassy clearing beside a dry, rocky drainage.

Past the next stand of trees is a broad **rockslide**. Ignore the 1.2-m (4-ft) cairn above. The trail stays low, curving around the base of the slide. Elevation: 1927 m (6320 ft).

Beyond the slide, enter forest whose aspect is softened by long-skirted spruce. Hop over a creeklet at 2055 m (6740 ft). An aggressive ascent ensues, but it's shorter than it appears.

Within 15 to 20 minutes, the grade eases above a cascade, beside a creeklet, at 2172 m (7126 ft). Big cliffs are visible across the valley. Castle Mtn is west. Five minutes farther, the trail curves east-southeast, approaching Mystic Pass.

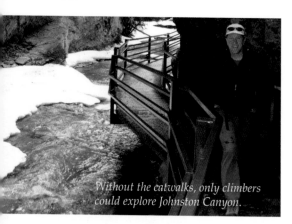

Without the catwalks, only climbers could explore Johnston Canyon.

Opportunity Alert: Stop where the trail levels at the northwest end of the pass, just before entering a narrow cleft with scree on both sides. Look left (northeast). See the game path climbing diagonally across the talus slope? It leads to the ridgecrest and affords an aerial view of the pass and the next valley. Think of it as dessert.

For now, finish the meal at hand by following the main trail south-southeast. Reach your destination, **Mystic Pass**, at 14.5 km (9 mi), 2280 m (7478 ft).

The trail continues south-southeast. It drops through subalpine meadows then forest to a T-junction in Mystic Valley at 17.5 km (10.9 mi), 1995 m (6545 ft). Left (east) descends 0.5 km (0.3 mi) to Mystic Valley campground. Right (west) ascends 0.5 km (0.3 mi) to Mystic Lake.

The lake is beyond dayhiking range for most. But if you have energy, curiosity and sufficient daylight, you might enjoy dessert. Scurry onto the aforementioned game path. It's steep but affords adequate footing. Follow it north to a 2500-m (8200-ft) dip on the **crest of the Sawback Range**.

Immediately below the far side of the crest is a tarn. Far below is Forty-Mile Creek Valley extending north-northwest and south-southeast. The Vermilion Range forms the valley's east wall.

trip 5

lake minnewanka
aylmer lookout
aylmer pass

location	northeast of Banff townsite
round trip	lakeshore 6 km (3.7 mi) to 16.4 km (10.2 mi)
	lookout 23.4 km (14.5 mi)
	pass 27 km (16.7 mi)
	lookout & pass 30.2 km (18.7 mi)
elevation gain	lakeshore 100 m (328 ft)
	lookout 662 m (2172 ft)
	pass 895 m (2936 ft)
	lookout and pass 1026 m (3366 ft)
key elevations	trailhead 1482 m (4862 ft)
	lookout 2052 m (6732 ft)
	pass 2285 m (7497 ft)
hiking time	1 to 4 hours for lakeshore
	7 to 8 hours for lookout
	10 to 11 hours for lookout and pass
difficulty	easy to challenging
	depending on distance
available	May through October
map	Gem Trek *Banff & Mt. Assiniboine*

opinion

Here in the Rockies, keen local hikers ache most of the year. Not from hiking, but from the unfulfilled desire to hike. Snowdrifts that could bury an NBA team keep hiking season cruelly short. Only after mid-July can you expect rock, not ice, to be crunching beneath your boots on the high passes.

Clematis

But there are a few special places where snow-free hiking is both possible and enjoyable in May. One of them is Lake Minnewanka, the 22-km (17-mi) long, fiord-like lake just northeast of Banff townsite.

Clinging to the lake's forested north shore is a trail where even a trifling effort rewards you with grand scenery. The enormous lake is often in view. So are the shriekingly steep cliffs of Mt. Inglismaldie, above the south shore. Yet the elevation gain is minimal for the first 7.8 km (4.8 mi), making this hike suitable for anyone.

Striding a mere 2.5 km (1.6 mi), or about 30 minutes, will earn you an immense panorama. Carry on and you'll soon have opportunities to scramble down to the rocky shore where you can appreciate the view in solitude, savour your bison sandwich and ginger snaps, and, if it's sunny, soak up your minimum daily requirement of Vitamin D.

It's cloudy? Rainy? Of all the Banff-area trails, this one's the most enjoyable in foul weather. Even when low-flying clouds are banging into the peaks, the lovely lake remains in view because it's below the trail.

Minnewanka, by the way, is a Stoney Indian name meaning *Water of the Spirits*. According to legend, the lake is haunted by fish-people. Aboriginal artifacts discovered here suggest human habitation 11,000 years ago.

The original, much smaller body of water was dammed to create today's reservoir. It's the only hydroelectric power source in a Canadian national park. Despite its vast surface area, the lake is only 97 m (318 ft) deep.

Energetic hikers will reach a lakeside campground in about two hours, at 7.8 km (4.8 mi). After a leisurely rest in this grassy, park-like setting, you can turn back or push on. **Aylmer lookout** is an hour and fifteen minutes farther, although just five minutes in that direction will greatly expand your view.

It's a stiff, 562-m (1844-ft) climb to the fire-lookout site atop a bluff. Bighorn sheep are just as prevalent now as they were when the lookout attendants set out salt blocks. The commanding lake-and-mountain view will have your eyes dangling from their springs. The lookout is a particularly exhilarating achievement for early season.

Lake Minnewanka, from Aylmer Lookout

Aylmer Pass is 3.4 km (2.1 mi) farther, 364 m (1194 ft) higher, and remains snowbound longer than the lookout. Yet the scenery is less dramatic. No lake view, no nearby imposing peaks. Just lots of rocks and tundra in a long, broad, alpine groove in the south end of the Palliser Range.

The extra time and effort to reach the pass is worthwhile, however, simply to experience the sharp sense of wilderness that such desolate, high-elevation settings invariably elicit. Plus the pass is usually hikeable by mid-June, when most passes in the Canadian Rockies have yet to shed their white winter coats.

The possibility of cresting a genuine pass so early in the summer is an irresistible invitation to any strong, serious hiker.

No way you'll reach both the lookout *and* the pass? Choose the lookout. And not just because the trail to the lookout is shorter and less steep. The upper elevations here in Banff Park's southern reaches are bleak, devoid of glaciers, deprived of greenery.

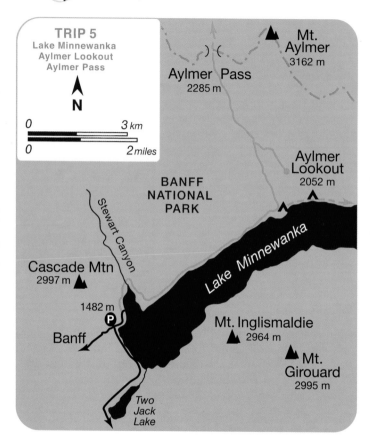

TRIP 5
Lake Minnewanka
Aylmer Lookout
Aylmer Pass

N

| 0 | | 3 km |
| 0 | | 2 miles |

Mt. Aylmer
3162 m

Aylmer Pass
2285 m

Aylmer Lookout
2052 m

BANFF NATIONAL PARK

Stewart Canyon

Lake Minnewanka

Cascade Mtn
2997 m

1482 m
P

Banff

Mt. Inglismaldie
2964 m

Mt. Girouard
2995 m

Two Jack Lake

So what you see from the pass is a vast expanse of gray. But the culminating sight at the lookout is the strident blue of Lake Minnewanka splashed across that grayness.

Fleet hikers can reach the lookout or the pass and return in a long day. Robo hikers can tag both in a one-day epic. To more comfortably achieve either of those goals, ride a mountain bike as far as the 7.8-km (4.8-mi) junction on the lakeshore trail. Then stash your bike and strap on your jet pack. The ascent is easy or merciless depending on your fitness level. The trail, however, is closed July 15 to Sept. 30 due to bears in the area.

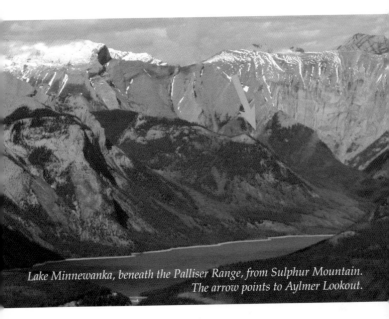

Lake Minnewanka, beneath the Palliser Range, from Sulphur Mountain. The arrow points to Aylmer Lookout.

Whatever your plan, before ascending from the Aylmer junction, guzzle and refill. Your choice of refreshments: stream or lake. Both require filtering. The ensuing climb can be a sweltering ordeal even in June. The next reliable water source is an hour or more up, up, up the trail.

Aylmer Lookout is on a southwest-facing, sun-exposed slope—dry and hot—which means it's tick habitat. In early summer, ambitious, scenery-seeking hikers might carry home a few insidious, bloodsucking ticks.

Don't let that stop you. Just remember to check the nape of your neck and your extremities after rest stops, then inspect your dark, secret recesses at day's end.

Think of it as an excuse to get intimate with your hiking partner: "Time for a tick inspection!"

Lake Minnewanka, from just above Aylmer Pass junction

by vehicle

From the Banff Park entrance near Canmore, drive Hwy 1 northwest toward Banff townsite. Take the first Banff townsite exit (right), also signed for Lake Minnewanka. At the stop sign, where left (south) goes under the highway to the townsite, turn right (north) onto the Lake Minnewanka Road.

Or, from Banff townsite, drive Banff Avenue (the main street) north out of town. After it passes under the Trans-Canada Hwy, it becomes the Lake Minnewanka Road.

From either approach, starting near the Trans-Canada underpass, drive the Lake Minnewanka Road north 5.5 km (3.4 mi) to the large, paved parking lot at 1482 m (4862 ft), just above the lake's west end.

The Lake Minnewanka Road is blocked? No worries. The trailhead is accessible year-round, despite the November 15 through April 15 road closure. Immediately before the barricade, turn right.

Follow signs for Two Jack Lake. Beyond Two Jack Lake Picnic Area, the road reaches the shore of Lake Minnewanka. Proceed northwest across the dam, into the parking lot described above.

on foot

Walk the paved service road generally east-northeast past the boat dock and through the picnic area.

After passing three cooking shelters, pavement ends and the signed trail begins at 0.6 km (0.4 mi). Proceed north on the wide, level, forest-enclosed path.

In about 20 minutes, at 1.5 km (0.9 mi), cross a bridge over **Stewart Canyon**. The Cascade River enters the lake via this fault in the limestone bedrock.

Above the river's east bank, a left spur leads up-canyon (northwest) 1.2 km (0.7 mi). Bear right, stay on the main trail, and begin the biggest ascent of the lakeshore hike: a mere 45 m (148 ft).

Sunbathing in May at Lake Minnewanka

Soon curve right (south-southeast). Cascade Mtn is visible right (west-southwest) through a forest of lodgepole and limber pine, Douglas fir, birch, and aspen. Look for lavender clematis here. You'll walk through an old burn for about 15 minutes.

At 2.5 km (1.6 mi), 1527 m (5010 ft), reach a **highpoint** overlooking the lake. Mt. Rundle, across the Bow Valley, dominates the southern horizon. The trail now traverses rocky ground, curving northeast up the lake.

A gentle descent ensues. For the next 20 minutes, the lake is constantly in sight. So is rugged Mt. Inglismaldie, above the south shore. Later, both are occasionally visible through the trees.

Continuing through open forest, the trail is mostly level, except for brief ups and downs. Cross a series of streambeds (usually dry).

About two hours from the parking lot, cross a footlog spanning Aylmer Creek. Just beyond, in a small, grassy clearing, reach signed **Aylmer Pass junction** at 7.8 km (4.8 mi), 1490 m (4888 ft).

Straight (east-northeast) continues paralleling the lakeshore. Left (north) climbs to Aylmer lookout and pass. Right (south-east) soon enters **LM8 campground** and ends at the lakeshore in 0.4 km (0.25 mi).

Aylmer Lookout

From **Aylmer Pass junction,** the trail ascends generally north-northwest at a moderate grade. Aylmer Lookout is 3.9 km (2.4 mi) distant and 562 m (1844 ft) above you. Aylmer Creek, in the gorge below, is audible. Blue clematis is prolific here. It creeps like a vine onto tree trunks and low branches, brightening the forest.

About 30 minutes above the junction, the trail levels at 1838 m (6030 ft). At 10.1 km (6.3 mi), 1921 m (6302 ft), reach **Aylmer Lookout fork** in a tiny clearing. Fit hikers will arrive here about 40 minutes after leaving Aylmer Pass junction. Straight (north) continues to Aylmer Pass. Turn right (northeast) to reach the lookout—1.6 km (1 mi) farther—in another 35 minutes.

At the lookout fork, refill your water containers. About 3 m /yd north of the fork, a very steep path descends left (west) to Aylmer Creek. Be cautious.

The lookout trail ascends from the fork, but it soon levels. Ten minutes farther it descends about 8 m (26 ft), then resumes climbing. About 30 minutes from the fork, it levels again, on an open slope. Lake Minnewanka is visible below.

After several switchbacks, reach the site of **Aylmer Lookout** at 11.7 km (7.3 mi), 2052 m (6732 ft). The lookout was dismantled in 1985. Only the cement footings remain.

Banff townsite and Tunnel Mtn are visible southwest. The north end of Mt. Rundle is south-southwest, above the Bow Valley. South, across the lake, are 2963-m (9721-ft) Mt. Inglismaldie and 2994-m (9823-ft) Mt. Girouard. A 10-km (6.2-mi) stretch of the lake is visible southeast before it bends out of sight.

Aylmer Pass

From **Aylmer Lookout fork**, at 10.1 km (6.3 mi), 1921 m (6302 ft), you'll gain 364 m (1194 ft) in 3.4 km (2.1 mi) to the crest of Aylmer Pass. The total ascent from Aylmer Pass junction, on the Lake Minnewanka trail, is 795 m (2608 ft) in 5.7 km (3.5 mi).

At the lookout fork, refill your water containers. About 3 m/yd north of the fork, a very steep path descends left (west) to Aylmer Creek. Be cautious.

Departing the lookout fork, proceed straight (north) for Aylmer Pass. The ascent remains earnest as you follow the trail up the forested canyon between Mt. Aylmer (right) and Mt. Astley (left).

About 30 minutes above the fork, enter the subalpine zone at 2010 m (6594 ft). The forest is now more open and the trees smaller. The ascent steepens.

Cross several lush avalanche paths, including one with a big rockslide. In early summer, expect to see cascades and wildflowers.

Globeflowers (creamy white, five petals, a central cluster of yellow stamens) are prominent. Also look for western spring-beauty (dainty, pink stripes, white petals).

Where the trail drops into an avalanche chute (possibly snow-filled in early summer), cross it then turn sharply left up the far side. A steep, tussocky, gravelly slope on the right indicates you're near the pass.

About an hour above the lookout fork, enter the alpine zone at 2200 m (7218 ft). The trail dips left into a gully then rises over a rockslide.

Reach the south end of 1.2-km (0.75-mi) long **Aylmer Pass** at 12.8 km (7.9 mi), 2265 m (7431 ft). In early summer, avoid snow by staying high on the talus-and-dryas-covered east slope.

Aylmer Pass

It might be convenient to abandon the trail by bearing right where it nips into a trough. Then proceed cross-country north-northeast until you can see down the north side of the pass.

If the area appears to be snow-free, however, stay on the trail and rockhop to the west bank of Aylmer Creek. Then follow an intermittent path ascending gently over scree about 0.7 km (0.4 mi) to the summit of Aylmer Pass, at 13.5 km (8.4 mi), 2285 m (7497 ft).

Apparition Mtn is visible north. Walling off the east side of the pass is 3161-m (10,371-ft) Mt. Aylmer. South-southeast, above Lake Minnewanka's far shore, is 2963-m (9721-ft) Mt. Inglismaldie. The austere, gray, limestone peaks of the Palliser Range are north-northwest.

Budgeting your time in hope of also visiting Aylmer Lookout? Swift hikers can descend from the summit of Aylmer Pass to Aylmer Lookout fork in about 40 minutes.

Western chaliceflower in Sunshine Meadows (Trip 6)

trip 6
⊕ citadel pass

location	southeast of Sunshine Ski Area
round trip	18.6 km (11.5 mi)
elevation gain	700 m (2296 ft)
key elevations	trailhead 2195 m (7200 ft)
	pass 2360 m (7740 ft)
hiking time	6 to 7 hours
difficulty	moderate
available	July through October
map	Gem Trek *Banff & Mt. Assiniboine*

opinion

The impact of skimming a heli-hiking brochure is double-barreled. First the photos. Then the price list. Both are breathtaking. But for those of us lacking hockey socks full of money, there's an alternative. An affordable way to be whisked up a mountain and begin hiking above timberline, in a see-forever alpine meadow. Simply catch the shuttle up to the ski area at Sunshine Village, where the trail to Citadel Pass offers maximal scenery in return for minimal elevation gain.

It's an idyllic hike through country that does a believable imitation of heaven, unless you're here during a thunderstorm. The meadows sprawl for 15 km (9 mi) near the crest of the Continental Divide. Mid-July through mid-August, you'll likely witness a vast array of wildflowers, which can make this an enjoyable outing even on a drizzly day. But tempestuous weather is no fun at this elevation, and could be dangerous, because you're totally exposed to whatever the sky throws at you. Besides, good visibility is essential for appreciating distant

views of mighty Mt. Assiniboine and other impressive peaks including The Monarch—a massive mountain whose dominant appearance justifies its name.

Don't zero-in on Howard Douglas Lake as a dayhike destination. It's in a shallow bowl that limits views. And you needn't climb Quartz Hill for an improved panorama. Follow the trail beyond it and the lake. Southeast of Quartz Hill, you can see the mountains it previously blocked. You'll face plenty of ups and downs just staying on the trail; adding cross-country exploration to your effort will make it exceedingly difficult to reach Citadel Pass and make it back to Sunshine Village in time to catch the last shuttle down to the parking lot. Though this trip begins in the alpine zone, your accumulated ascent by day's end will be substantial. The elevation gain stated above is a conservative estimate only.

Swift dayhikers, taking advantage of the gentle terrain, can stride out, reaching Citadel Pass in 2½ hours—if they're not detained by a brilliant flower display. The benefit of a fast pace is that you can extend the trip beyond Citadel, to Fatigue Pass. Just 15 minutes beyond, the magic of a little ascent will reveal itself. Distant peaks seem to leap into the foreground. Mt. Assiniboine is south/southeast. U-shaped Wonder Pass is left (northeast) of Mt. Assiniboine. Nasswald Peak and Og Mtn are southeast. Fatigue Mtn is nearby, northeast. Even Mt. Temple is visible, northwest. Simpson Ridge is southwest. Try to allow an extra hour for this additional scenery splurge.

If you balk at the cost of riding the shuttle, it's possible to hoof it from the Sunshine parking lot up to Sunshine Village. The distance: 6.5 km (4 mi). The ascent: 520 m (1706 ft). It takes at least 1½ hours. It's boring, too. Just a rocky road switchbacking up through trees. And remember, you'd have to hike back down as well. Even if you're very fit, it's worth paying for the shuttle. Think of all the long, sweaty ascents you've cursed. This is a rare opportunity to skip one. Take it.

Western chaliceflower and fireweed.
Quartz Hill in background.

fact

The convenience of shuttle service to these extraordinary alp-lands assures you won't be alone. But a choice of destinations, people's widely varying hiking speeds, and the sheer vastness of the terrain will allow you more solitude than you might expect.

The Sunshine Meadows area draws an average of 60 visitors on a sunny, summer day; sometimes as many as 130. But 60% mosey no farther than Rock Isle or Grizzly lakes, so you won't see too many trekking to Citadel Pass, or Healy Pass (Trip 8). A mere 10% of visitors are backpackers heading to Assiniboine. If you're here to hike (as opposed to walk), you can leave most people behind at or before Howard Douglas Lake.

The profusion of wildflowers belies the harshness of this sky-high environment. It provides only 45 growing days per year. Some plants struggle 20 years to produce a single flower. Help

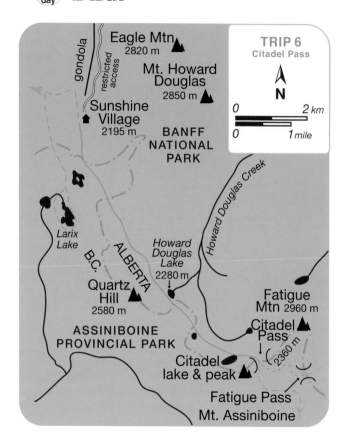

preserve these hardy-yet-delicate beings by not plucking them or crushing them under foot. Stay on the trails.

before your trip

Visit www.sunshinemeadowsbanff.com to check the current schedule and prices for the shuttle bus operated by White Mountain Adventures (www.whitemountainadventures.com) that runs between the Sunshine Ski Area parking lot and Sunshine Village. The ticket office (403-762-7889) is open June through September.

by vehicle

Drive the Trans-Canada Hwy east 21 km (13 mi) from Castle Junction, or west 9 km (5.6 mi) from Banff townsite. Turn south onto the road signed for Sunshine Ski Area. Proceed 8.3 km (5.1 mi) to the parking lot near the gondola station, at 1675 m (5495 ft). The gondola does not operate in summer.

by bus

In the past, the first bus (mid-June through August only, advance purchase required) has departed at 8 a.m. Starting at 9 a.m. (mid-June through September, no reservations necessary) buses have departed approximately every hour, with the last bus up at 4:45 p.m. Return times have also been approximately every hour, with the last bus down at 5:30 p.m. If you ride the first bus up, then hike like a demon, it's possible to reach Fatigue Pass and return to the village in time to catch the last bus down. If the shuttle schedule is too restrictive for you, ask about one-way prices.

on foot

From Sunshine Village ski lodge, at 2195 m (7200 ft), walk south past the left (east) side of the saloon. Go uphill 200 m (220 yd) to the Parks Canada cabin. Fifteen meters past it, turn left (east-southeast) onto the well-groomed gravel path. It ascends gently.

Reach the first junction at 2290 m (7510 ft). Go right (south) and continue the easy ascent. In another 5-7 minutes, reach the next junction, 1.2 km (0.7 mi) from the village. Right (west) leads to Rock Isle Lake. Go left (south-southeast) on the narrower path for Quartz Hill and Citadel Pass.

The north end of Quartz Hill is visible south. Wedgwood Peak and other giants in the Assiniboine area are south-southeast. Lookout Mtn is the gray peak northeast with a ski lift on its bare chest. Mt. Howard Douglas looms above it. Behind it is Brewster Creek Valley.

About 45 minutes from the village, the trail descends—one of many downs and ups. Soon regain 145 m (480 ft). Much of the narrow path is deeply eroded through here.

If the wildflower show hasn't slowed you, reach a 2393-m (7850-ft) shoulder of **Quartz Hill** in about 1½ hours, having hiked 5 km (3 mi) from the village.

The 3618-m (11,867-ft) horn of Mt. Assiniboine is visible ahead. The first lake beneath you is Howard Douglas. Citadel Pass is the cleft way left (east-southeast)—not the lower, forested saddle south-southeast.

Descend to reach the shore of **Howard Douglas Lake** at 2280 m (7480 ft). There's a treed campground behind the lake's northeast corner.

After the deeply rutted, narrow trail to Howard Douglas, the path improves through meadows with a scattering of alpine fir and larch. Ascend 100 m (330 ft) and pass another lake before reaching **Citadel Pass** at 9.3 km (5.8 mi), 2360 m (7740 ft).

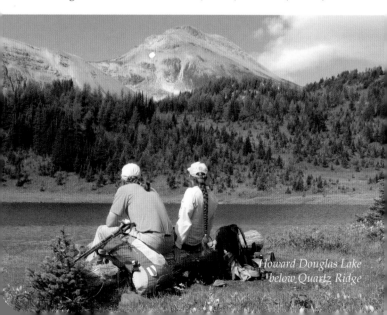

Howard Douglas Lake below Quartz Ridge

Fatigue Pass

Citadel Peak is right (southwest). Fatigue Mtn is left (northeast). A big sign here indicates you're about to enter Mt. Assiniboine Provincial Park. Another sign by the Banff Park kiosk has ridiculously varying distances. Magog Lake, at the base of Mt. Assiniboine, is 19.6 km (12.2 mi) southeast, though one sign says 17 km.

If proceeding to Fatigue Pass, ascend left (east) from the Assiniboine sign. Fatigue is only 2.5 km (1.6 mi) beyond Citadel Pass, and if all you want is a better view you don't even have to go that far.

Though you can initially pick up a faint path, it peters out. Look southeast and you'll see where it resumes, switchbacking up a rounded, grassy mound. Continue in that direction, over heather, through a draw, and across a rockslide.

Shortly after tagging onto the trail you saw from Citadel Pass, it too disappears. But there are now widely spaced cairns to guide you. Rise to 2470 m (8100 ft), then drop into 2390-m (7840-ft) **Fatigue Pass**.

Ambitious scramblers can choose a route from just north of Citadel Pass, to the summit of 2959-m (9707-ft) Fatigue Mtn.

trip 7

cory and edith passes

location	northwest of Banff townsite
round trip	11 km (6.8 mi) to Cory Pass
circuit	12.9 km (8 mi) around Mt. Edith
elevation gain	900 m (2952 ft) to Cory Pass
	1000 m (3280 ft) on circuit
key elevations	trailhead 1460 m (4789 ft)
	Cory Pass 2360 m (7741 ft)
	Edith Pass 1950 m (6396 ft)
hiking time	4½ to 6 hours for circuit
difficulty	moderate
available	mid-July through October
map	Gem Trek *Banff Up-Close*

opinion

Snow must have talons, it clings so tenaciously. But if you're in Banff townsite, eager to hike, and the snow won't go, here's one option: Cory Pass.

Southern exposure and quick access make Cory worth trying in mid-June. Even if snow-filled gullies bar your final ascent, completing the first 3 km (1.9 mi) is worthwhile. You'll be high on a ridge, with the rugged walls of Mounts Cory and Edith above you, and views south to the Sundance Range. After late June, attaining the pass is a realistic goal.

It's an exhilarating trip. An 885-m (2903-ft) gain in just 4.5 km (2.8 mi) will place shocking demands on lethargic muscles. The trail is airy, dropping steeply away on one side; definitely not for acrophobes. Rock pinnacles give the pass a feral atmosphere. And just beyond the pass, the fang-like 500-m (1640-ft) face of Mt. Louis looms like a monster in a child's

The trail to Cory Pass

nightmare. The first person to climb it was Conrad Kain, sort of the Captain Cook of the Canadian Rockies.

When snow has lost its grip on the north side of Cory Pass, perhaps by mid-July, you can complete a circuit. From Cory, drop into the appropriately named Gargoyle Valley, round the talusy north side of Mt. Edith, then return via forested Edith Pass. Edith isn't scenic, but the circuit adds variety and allows a more comfortable, gradual descent.

Get smart before you depart. You'll be grappling with rugged terrain, traversing slopes that are sayonara steep. With no switchbacks, the ascent is abusive. It will waste anyone inexperienced or unfit. If you turn around at Cory Pass, expect a toe-jamming descent. If you're insecure on steep, loose rock, the route into Gargoyle Valley will rattle you. But these challenges only make the trip more interesting for capable hikers. Regardless of your confidence, don't brave any snow crossings that appear dangerous—because they are. And pack full water bot-

Descending into Gargoyle Valley

tles; it's dry up there. The worst aspect of this trip is noise. For a long way, you'll hear the distressing racket of vehicles speeding on the Trans-Canada.

fact

by vehicle

From where Bow Valley Parkway (Highway 1A) departs the Trans-Canada Highway, just west of Banff townsite, drive the Parkway north 0.5 km (0.3 mi). Then turn right onto the access road for the Fireside Picnic Area. Continue 1 km (0.6 mi) to road's end. The trailhead is near the bridge over the creek, at 1460 m (4789 ft).

on foot

Cross the bridge and pass the picnic area. Head east, initially on an old road. In 200 m (220 yd) follow a trail left (marked by a hiker sign). It leads through forest lightened by aspen and broken by meadows. At 1 km (0.6 mi), the trail to Edith Pass continues straight. If you complete the circuit, you'll return that way from Edith. Go left (north) for Cory Pass.

The Cory Pass trail climbs skyward, generally northwest, up the south-facing slope. Crest the forested south ridge of Mt. Edith at 1900 m (6232 ft), having hiked just over 2 km (1.2 mi). Rewarding views begin. Mt. Bourgeau (Trip 9) is southwest. The Sundance Range is south. Mt. Rundle is southeast. The trail bends north-northwest and the ascent eases. Ahead is

2553-m (8374-ft) Mt. Edith. Northwest is 2801-m (9187-ft) Mt. Cory. Between them is Cory Pass.

The trail follows the ridgeline, continuing at a moderate grade with one steep stretch. At 2045 m (6707 ft), it drops 14 m (45 ft) into an awkward declivity, then ascends gradually across the barren southwest slope of **Mt. Edith**. This long, airy traverse is on a very narrow trail. It crosses several rocky, avalanche chutes that can clutch snow until July. These spots are precarious even when snowfree. Traverse the canyon headwall to reach the narrow defile of **Cory Pass** at 5.5 km (3.4 mi), 2360 m (7741 ft).

Mt. Louis, from Cory Pass

Directly north, across Gargoyle Valley, is 2682-m (8797-ft) Mt. Louis. Mt. Fifi is north-northwest.

To continue the Cory-Edith circuit, descend the precipitous north side of the pass. The trail curves right (northeast), dropping rapidly across steep talus through short **Gargoyle Valley**. Rounding the north side of Mt. Edith, stay high, just beneath the cliffs. You'll see gargoyle pinnacles through here. Closely follow the cairns through bulky rubble. Near 2000 m (6560 ft), the trail works its way right (southeast). Maintain your elevation while crossing a boulder field for ten minutes. Then watch for a yellow-orange hiker sign on a tree; that's where the trail enters forest.

Mt. Fifi ▲

Forty Mile
Creek

Mt. ▲
Louis
2682 m

Gargoyle
Valley

Mt.Cory
2800 m ▲

▲ Mt.
Edith

Cory
Pass
2360 m

▲
Mt.
Norquay
2515 m

TRIP 7
Cory and
Edith Passes

↑
N

0   2 km
0   1 mile

BANFF
NATIONAL
PARK

Banff

1460 m Ⓟ

1A

Castle Jct.

Ascend then descend yet again before reaching 1950-m (6396-ft) **Edith Pass** at 9 km (5.6 mi). Mt. Edith is now west, Mt. Norquay east. Trails depart both sides of Edith Pass. Don't turn left (north), or you'll drop to the Forty Mile Creek trail. Go right (south), and descend—steeply at first, then moderately—through forest. Reach a junction at 11.9 km (7.4 mi). You're now on familiar ground. Right leads north to Cory Pass. Straight leads 1 km (0.6 mi) generally south-southwest back to the trailhead.

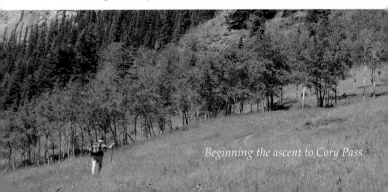

Beginning the ascent to Cory Pass

healy pass / monarch ramparts

location	northwest of Sunshine ski area
round trip	18.4 km (11.4 mi) plus 8.4 km (5.2 mi) for Ramparts
elevation gain	655 m (2150 ft) from Sunshine parking lot to pass
	360 m (1180 ft) from Sunshine Village to pass
key elevations	Sunshine parking lot 1675 m (5495 ft)
	Sunshine Village 2195 m (7200 ft)
	Healy Pass 2330 m (7642 ft)
	Monarch Ramparts 2410 m (7905 ft)
hiking time	6 to 7 hours
difficulty	moderate
available	July through October
map	Gem Trek *Banff & Mt. Assiniboine*

opinion

Wildflower meadows, like coral reefs, have an enchanting power to rivet your attention to the present moment. In a culture preoccupied with the past and future, hiking or snorkeling can be therapeutic.

So hike to Healy Pass during full bloom—late July to mid-August—when the meadows are a riot of colour, as brilliantly and variously hued as a reef teeming with tropical fish. Your eyes will swim through bold splashes of red, pink, yellow, purple and white.

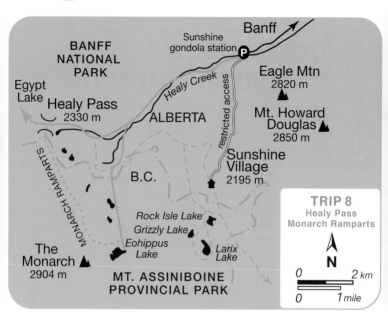

Even if the flower display is less than full strength, Healy Pass pleases. The view is grand, encompassing a 70-km (43.5-mi) length of the Continental Divide—from Mt. Assiniboine (south-east) to Storm Mtn (northwest). The Ball Range, the Pharaoh Peaks, and the Massive Range are prominently visible. You'll also see Egypt, Scarab, and Pharaoh lakes in context—more impressive than from their shorelines. In autumn, the pass again makes a spectacle of itself, sporting a brilliant gold beard of alpine larches.

Compared to most passes, Healy is generous. It offers hikers a sensational yet easy way to extend the day's exploration: continue along the 4.2-km (2.6-mi) alpine crest of the Monarch Ramparts. From the pass, the elevation gain is piddling. And views are constant. You can go out and back, or create a circuit by returning on the Eohippus Lake trail.

There are several ways to reach Healy Pass. These are the optimal choices: (1) Ride the shuttle bus up to Sunshine Village,

Monarch Ramparts and The Monarch, from Healy Pass

effortlessly gaining 520 m (1705 ft), then hike to Healy Pass via Simpson Pass. (2) From the Sunshine parking lot, hike to Healy Pass via Healy Creek.

Both approaches are virtually the same length. The ascent is four times greater on the Healy Creek trail, but the grade is moderate overall. The Healy Creek trail is also viewless, but the trail is periodically close to the creek. Stretches of the trail from Sunshine are often muddy.

If you're fit, hike up Healy Creek. You won't be restricted to the shuttle schedule, and you'll save money. If you don't mind the expense, ride the shuttle, hike in via Simpson, out via Healy Creek.

Trying to decide between Citadel Pass (Trip 6) and Healy Pass? Go to Citadel. You'll spend the entire day in open, alpine country, and you'll hike through more extensive meadows.

 **Banff**

fact

before your trip

Visit www.sunshinemeadowsbanff.com to check the current schedule and prices for the shuttle bus operated by White Mountain Adventures (www.whitemountainadventures.com) that runs between the Sunshine Ski Area parking lot and Sunshine Village. The ticket office (403-762-7889) is open June through September.

by vehicle

Drive the Trans-Canada Hwy east 21 km (13 mi) from Castle Junction, or west 9 km (5.6 mi) from Banff townsite. Turn south onto the signed Sunshine Village road. Proceed 8.3 km (5.1 mi) to the parking lot near the gondola station, at 1675 m (5495 ft). The gondola does not operate in summer.

(1) To reach Sunshine Village, at 2195 m (7200 ft), you must hike the restricted-use access road (starting on the south side of the gondola station), or ride the White Mountain Adventures shuttle bus. For details read the *by bus* section in Trip 6.

(2) To hike the Healy Creek trail, walk around the right (north) side of the gondola station. Enter the smaller parking lot behind. The trail, initially a road, starts left of the info kiosk. Elevation: 1675 m (5495 ft).

on foot

Starting at Sunshine Village

From the north end of the lodge, at 2195 m (7200 ft), turn left on the road. Proceed onto the gravel path. Go past the staff lodging to the trail sign at the bottom of Wawa Ridge ski lift. Follow the Meadow Park trail northwest uphill through subalpine forest. Bear right at the 1.6-km (1-mi) junction. Crest Wawa Ridge at 2 km (1.2 mi), 2360 m (7740 ft). From here you can see southeast to Sunshine Meadows, the Citadel Pass area, and Mt. Assiniboine.

Glacier lilies below Monarch Ramparts, early July

From Wawa Ridge, the trail drops west back into forest. After curving southwest, the descent steepens as you approach **Simpson Pass**. Reach the pass at 5.6 km (3.5 mi), 2135 m (7003 ft). It's a small meadow surrounded by forest. Pay attention at this potentially confusing junction:

• Right leads north 1.3 km (0.8 mi) to the Healy Creek trail, where you could descend right (northeast) 5.9 km (3.7 mi) to the Sunshine parking lot. That would spare you the 225-m (738-ft) ascent back to Wawa Ridge.

• For Healy Pass, bear left (west), climbing steeply. At 6 km (3.7 mi) ignore the left spur. It leads south 3.2 km (2 mi) to small Eohippus Lake. Your trail levels, then drops slightly to a junction with the Healy Creek trail at 7.6 km (4.7 mi). Bear left (northwest) and ascend into the tarn-sequined, flower-rich meadows north of the Monarch Ramparts. Crest 2330-m (7642-ft) **Healy Pass** at 9.1 km (5.6 mi).

Skip below for a description of the pass and directions to the Monarch Ramparts.

Starting at Sunshine parking lot

Behind (west of) the gondola station, the Healy Creek trail (initially a road) starts left of the info kiosk. Cross the culvert and begin ascending. For the first seven minutes, your road is beneath and parallel to the Sunshine Village access road. Healy Creek is below (right).

At 0.8 km (0.5 mi), 1765 m (5790 ft), a road ascends left. Descend right (southwest) on trail. A minute farther, cross a bridge over Sunshine Creek. The trail remains wide.

At 3 km (1.9 mi) cross a bridge to the north bank of **Healy Creek** and continue southwest. An hour from the trailhead, begin a noticeable but easy ascent. Fifteen minutes farther, a meadow of willow and shrubby cinquefoil breaks the forest.

At 5.4 km (3.3 mi) **Healy Creek campground** is on the left. The creek, 30 m/yd distant, is audible. The open forest of predominantly spruce is interspersed with willows and grassy meadow.

Reach a fork at 5.9 km (3.7 mi), 1982 m (6500 ft). Bear right (west) for Healy Pass. The ascent steepens. Left crosses a bridge over Healy Creek and leads south to Simpson Pass. You'll return to this fork from Simpson Pass if you complete the Monarch Ramparts / Eohippus Lake circuit.

At 7.7 km (4.8 mi) enter another **meadow** and reach a junction 20 m/yd past a bridge. Left leads south to Simpson Pass. Go right, heading northwest into the tarn-sequined, flower-rich meadows north of the Monarch Ramparts. The trail levels at 2134 m (7000 ft).

Crest 2330-m (7642-ft) **Healy Pass** at 9.2 km (5.7 mi). Fast hikers will be here 2½ hours after departing the trailhead. Southeast is 3618-m (11,867-ft) Mt. Assiniboine—30 km (19 mi) distant. South, at the far end of the Monarch Ramparts, is the 2904-m (9525-ft) pyramid called The Monarch. West-northwest are

Healy Pass meadows

Egypt and Scarab lakes. Northwest is Pharaoh Lake, beneath the Pharaoh Peaks. Northeast is the Massive Range, including Mt. Brett left and Mt. Bourgeau (Trip 9) right.

From Healy Pass, the **Monarch Ramparts** extend southeast 4.2 km (2.6 mi) to the base of The Monarch. A bootbeaten route runs along the crest of this 2410-m (7905-ft) high ridge. Fast hikers can dispatch it, out and back, in 2¼ hours. But with a little cross-country experience and preferably a map in hand, you don't have to turn around. Keep going. Descend the southeast end of the Ramparts to the tarn-dotted meadows below and complete a 25.2-km (15.6-mi) circuit via Simpson Pass.

If hiking the circuit, don't bail off the Ramparts too soon. The left (northeast) side of the ridge is forbiddingly steep for most of its length. Only near the end, beneath The Monarch, is the descent comfortably gradual. Here, a path among the larch and boulders invites passage to the meadows below. Expect to see a profusion of glacier lilies if you come in early July.

Near Healy Pass

Having successfully dismounted the ridge, you'll find the route fades in the meadows. Proceed southeast about 1 km (0.6 mi) to intersect a trail above the north shore of **Eohippus Lake**. Turn left and follow it north.

Reach a junction in 3.2 km (2 mi). Left (west) leads to Healy Pass. Go right. A 7-minute descent east leads to a signed junction in 2135-m (7003-ft) **Simpson Pass**. Straight (east) goes to Sunshine Meadows via Wawa Ridge. Turn left (northeast).

A steep, 1.3-km (0.8-mi) descent north ensues. Within 15 minutes, cross a bridge over **Healy Creek** and intersect the Healy Creek trail at 1982 m (6500 ft). You're now on familiar ground. Turn right. Descend the Healy Creek trail generally northeast 5.9 km (3.7 mi) to the Sunshine parking lot.

bourgeau lake
harvey pass
mt. bourgeau

location	west of Banff townsite
round trip	19.2 km (12 mi) to pass
	24 km (14.9 mi) to summit
elevation gain	1046 m (3431 ft) to pass
	1530 m (5018 ft) to summit
key elevations	trailhead 1401 m (4596 ft)
	lake 2150 m (7052 ft)
	pass 2447 m (8025 ft)
	summit 2931 m (9615 ft)
hiking time	5 to 7 hours for pass, 6 to 8 for summit
difficulty	moderate to pass
	challenging to summit
	due only to elevation gain
available	mid-July through September
map	Gem Trek *Banff & Mt. Assiniboine*

opinion

Bourgeau Lake is merely the box office. Harvey Pass is the warm-up act. Mt. Bourgeau is the headliner. Most people pay for a ticket, then leave without seeing the show. What they miss is astounding.

Atop Mt. Bourgeau's broad summit, you'll appreciate much of Banff National Park: sprawling meadows beneath you, icy peaks parading over distant horizons. Though the panorama is comparable to that afforded by Mt. Temple (the mammoth peak towering above Lake Louise), scrambling is not required

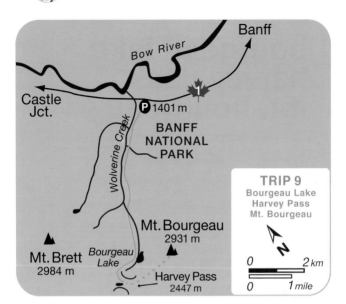

here. A discernible trail ascends from Harvey Pass, all the way up Bourgeau's west ridge. Given fair weather and sufficient daylight, you simply need the will and energy to keep walking. From the pass, robust hikers storm the peak in just 45 minutes.

The only obstacle that might foil your intent to summit Mt. Bourgeau is the superlative view from Harvey Pass. It's tempting to stop here. Mt. Assiniboine and the knot of burly bodyguard peaks surrounding it are an awesome sight; on clear days Harvey Pass offers a premier vantage of this grand massif. The expansive Sunshine and Healy Pass meadows are also visible from Harvey Pass and will keep your eyes happily roaming while you savour your Ryvita and smoked wild salmon.

Okay, you've finished lunch. Can't muster the resolve to continue ascending Mt. Bourgeau? How about a small burst of energy propelling you up the slope west-northwest of Harvey Pass? Minimal gain at a moderate grade soon grants an improved prospect. It might entice you to keep wandering the alplands toward Healy Pass—an off-trail excursion for which a map and

Mt. Bourgeau, from the shore of Bourgeau Lake

compass are helpful. And if that sounds too demanding, try departing Harvey Pass as if aiming for Mt. Bourgeau. Within minutes, at the first broad saddle, veer left. You'll quickly top out on the gentle knoll above Harvey Lake's northeast shore.

Just can't pry your posterior off that comfy perch in Harvey Pass? Fine. But make sure you get at least that far. Bourgeau Lake, beneath the massive, soaring northwest wall of Mt. Bourgeau, is impressively beautiful, yet even a swift hiker will plod nearly two hours through forest to get there and see nothing memorable en route. So take a break at the lake, then continue. Just above are lovely lakelets in an alpine basin. Between them is a cascading stream, where you'll enjoy the optimal, aerial view of Bourgeau Lake. And minutes above the second lakelet is Harvey Lake in Harvey Pass, where your sense of accomplishment, and the scenic reward for your effort, will increase exponentially.

fact

by vehicle

Drive the Trans-Canada Hwy west 2.8 km (1.7 mi) from the Sunshine Ski Area turnoff, or east 44 km (27.3 mi) from the Lake Louise turnoff. The trailhead is on the southwest side of the divided highway. If driving east, simply turn off right. If driving west, slow down, turn left, then stop before carefully crossing the east-bound lane. The trailhead parking lot is at 1401 m (4596 ft).

on foot

The trail departs the west end of the paved parking lot. A fence (built to prevent animal deaths on the highway) requires you to step up to a gate, then step back down to the trail. Pass the trail-head sign and head west.

In about 12 minutes, the trail approaches **Wolverine Creek canyon**, where the sound of rushing water drowns out the noise of vehicles on the highway. Your general direction of travel is now southwest and will remain so all the way to Bourgeau Lake.

Meadows northwest of Harvey Pass. Mt. Bourgeau in distance.

About 35 minutes from the trailhead, having ascended 230 m (754 ft), attain the first view: northwest into Wolverine Creek canyon and north-northeast across Bow Valley. The ascent eases. Views temporarily open.

After hiking about an hour, cross a bridge over a tributary stream at 3.7 km (2.3 mi). The gentle grade continues for about another half hour, until the trail reaches cascading **Wolverine Creek**, at 5.5 km (3.4 mi), 1850 m (6068 ft). Rockhop across, then begin ascending steeply.

About 15 minutes farther, just above the cascade, attain your first glimpse upward into **Bourgeau Lake basin**. Behind you, the view across Bow Valley has also expanded. The trail continues tilting skyward. You'll ascend another 10 minutes before it levels at 2108 m (6915 ft) then rolls into the subalpine zone. You've entered the basin. The wall of Mount Bourgeau looms ahead, south-southwest.

Expect mucky sections of trail here. (Stay on the main path. Mud won't hurt your boots, but straying off the trail will permanently widen it to an unsightly road width.) Reach the northeast shore of **Bourgeau Lake** at 7.4 km (4.6 mi), 2150 m (7052 ft). Near the shore, a sign indicates the trail to Harvey Pass.

The lakeshore is home to pesky, obese chipmunks who've learned that hikers are easy marks. If you take your pack off, keep it zipped shut. And steel yourself to the begging antics of these ravenous rogues. Processed food is even less nutritious for animals than it is for you. Feeding them erodes their ability to survive in the wild by fostering dependence on humans. Besides, feeding wild animals is illegal in the Canadian Rockies.

Proceeding to Harvey Pass? Good on you. From the sign near where you arrived at the lakeshore, follow the trail right (west-southwest). After rounding the lake's northwest shore (usually mucky), the trail improves as it ascends the right (north) side of the **inlet cascade**. Do not ascend the steep, narrow, slippery path above the cascade's south bank.

About 30 minutes after departing Bourgeau Lake, crest the lip of the upper basin and arrive at the **first lakelet**. Elevation: 2332 m (7650 ft). The trail continues around the north shore. Maintain a brisk pace and within five minutes you'll be rockhopping the creeklet draining the **second lakelet**. Follow the trail southeast now—above the first lakelet, just east of the second lakelet, up a short, steep, compacted scree slope—and another five minutes will bring you to the third

Moss Campion

lakelet, called **Harvey Lake**, in 2447-m (8025-ft) **Harvey Pass**, at 9.6 km (6 mi). Looking back, a tarn is now visible below, just above the second lakelet. But even this improved aerial view of the picturesque alpine basin doesn't compare with the wondrous vision ahead (south-southeast): the Mt. Assiniboine massif.

The trail rounds Harvey Lake's east shore. Within a couple minutes, reach the south side of Harvey Pass, where

Mt. Bourgeau summit ridge, from Harvey Pass

you have two options: (1) ascend left (east) for Mt. Bourgeau, or (2) follow a diminishing path right (southwest) onto heathery slopes. The trail up Mt. Bourgeau's west ridge is visible from the pass.

At an aggressive pace, it takes 45 minutes to hike from Harvey Pass to the top of 2931 m (9615 ft) **Mt. Bourgeau**. Distance from the trailhead: 12 km (7.5 mi). The day's total elevation gain: 1530 m (5018 ft). Though a small communications structure crowns the mountain, the summit is spacious and the panorama is unmarred. On a clear day, you can spend an hour identifying significant Canadian Rockies landmarks. A sampling of the spectacle includes Banff townsite (east-northeast), Mt. Joffre and the big peaks in Kananaskis Country (distant southeast), Mt. Assiniboine (south-southeast), Sunshine Meadows and Ski Area (south), Healy Pass (southwest), the Bugaboos (distant southwest), Mt. Ball (west-northwest), Mt. Temple and the big peaks between Lake Louise and Lake O'Hara (northwest).

Strong, determined hikers can return to the trailhead within three hours of departing the summit.

trip 10

cascade mountain

location	immediately north of Banff townsite
round trip	21 km (13 mi)
elevation gain	1557 m (5108 ft)
key elevations	trailhead 1700 m (5577 ft)
	Forty Mile Creek 1570 m (5151 ft)
	Cascade Amphitheatre 2125 m (6972 ft)
	summit 2997 m (9833 ft)
hiking time	9 hours
difficulty	challenging
available	August through September
map	Gem Trek *Banff Up-Close*

opinion

Relaxing isn't the best way to relax.

No matter how wet the coaster is you've been setting your cold ones on, a sweaty brow is a better indication you're truly relaxed.

Still, most people leave their cubicles Friday afternoon hoping that on Monday morning, when asked "How was your week-end?" they can say "Oh, it was really relaxing."

But after achieving that slothful goal, if asked a few days later what they did, they have difficulty recounting even the slightest detail. That's the other problem with relaxation. It's utterly forgettable.

So here's an ambitious hike you'll remember vividly years later: an ascent of the monumental peak looming just beyond the end of Banff Avenue.

Ascending Cascade Mountain above Elk Valley

Lift your eyes while walking north along the sidewalk, and Cascade Mountain fills the horizon, making this the most spectacular thoroughfare in Canada.

The sheer southeast face is visible when entering Banff Park from Canmore. This is where you'll see the cascades—water in summer, ice in winter—that spawned the mountain's name.

This is also the side that lures all manner of would-be assailants, from talented ice-climbers to naive tourists. Each year, a few plummet to their death or, if they're lucky, are plucked off the face by a rescue posse.

But you needn't make your summit bid *that* memorable. The mountain's west side is benign. Here, a trail leads 6.4 km (4 mi) to Cascade Amphitheatre. You can then follow a route—occasionally cairned, often distinct, entirely obvious to experienced scramblers—4.1 km (2.5 mi) to the top.

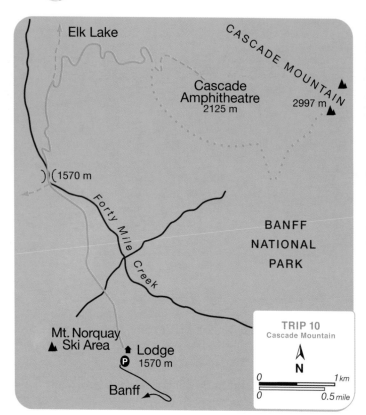

Elk Lake

CASCADE MOUNTAIN

Cascade
Amphitheatre
2125 m

2997 m

)(1570 m

BANFF

NATIONAL

PARK

Forty Mile Creek

Mt. Norquay
▲ Ski Area   ▲ Lodge
    Ⓟ 1570 m

Banff

TRIP 10
Cascade Mountain

↑
N

0   1 km
0   0.5 mile

That's not to say this is an easy outing. By the time you return
to the trailhead you'll have ascended nearly a vertical mile.
The upper half of the hike is rough and steep. Even if you
can dance like Pan on vertiginous terrain—boulders, talus,
ledges—you're in for a nine-hour day.

The culminating panorama is spectacular. Lake Minnewanka,
the Bow Valley, and Banff townsite are below. A great swath of
southern Banff Park's famous topography is within view.

The real reward, however, is en route: the fun challenge of
tracing the mountain's musculature. Soon after departing the

The col below the summit of Cascade Mountain

amphitheatre mouth, the scenery opens up and the terrain begins changing.

What you'll likely find hardest about this trip is the trail to the amphitheatre. Swift striders dispatch it in an hour-and-a-half, but it's viewless. You'll see little but spindly lodgepole pine and spruce trees. So choose an entertaining companion.

Don't bother detouring into the amphitheatre. With no lake and only a small subalpine meadow, it's of little interest. The wildflower display can be winsome—yellow glacier lilies in late June—but doesn't justify the boring approach. Besides, blossoms are out of the question if your goal is Cascade Mountain, which usually isn't snow-free and safely hikeable until August.

The days are getting shorter then, so start your hike early. You'll want to linger long on the summit—marveling at the panorama, savouring your accomplishment, and yes, relaxing—without having to race the setting sun back to the trailhead.

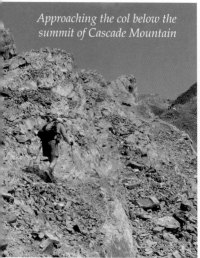

Approaching the col below the summit of Cascade Mountain

Final ascent to the summit of Cascade Mountain

fact

before your trip

You're in for a long day, and the mountain is dry as a law-abiding town during Prohibition, so pack three litres of water per person.

by vehicle

From Banff townsite's west interchange on the Trans-Canada Hwy, ascend the switchbacking Mt. Norquay Road north 5.8 km (3.6 mi) to the far end of the ski-area parking lot. The trail, initially a road, leads between the ski lodge buildings, at 1700 m (5577 ft).

on foot

Walk the dirt road north. Pass the Cascade chairlift. About eight minutes from the ski lodge, signed trail begins right of (behind and below) the Spirit chairlift. Follow it north. Do not go right over the bridge onto the Stoney Squaw bridal path.

About 15 minutes from the parking lot, at 1655 m (5430 ft), continue the gradual descent right of the Mystic chairlift. Drop deeper into forest.

Reach a junction at 2.4 km (1.5 mi). Left (west) is the Forty Mile Creek trail heading upstream toward Mystic Lake. Go right (northeast) and descend.

A minute farther, at 1570 m (5151 ft), cross a bridge over **Forty Mile Creek**. You've lost 130 m (427 ft) since leaving the trailhead. Begin a moderate ascent north.

About an hour from the trailhead, reach a junction at 3.8 km (2.4 mi), 1725 m (5659 ft). Left leads north to Elk Lake. Go right (northeast). Begin a steep, switchbacking ascent generally east through scraggly forest.

About 30 minutes farther, the trail enters the mouth of **Cascade Amphitheatre** at 6.4 km (4 mi), 2125 m (6972 ft). You can continue about 1 km (0.6 mi) into the amphitheatre, but why? You'll see it from above on your way to the summit.

The route to Cascade Mtn starts just outside the amphitheatre mouth. At the meadow's edge, turn around and walk back 155 paces. Turn left (south) onto a bootbeaten path that might still be crudely blocked by logs.

This well-trod spur ascends south-southeast through forest onto the **ridge** forming Cascade Amphitheatre's southwest wall. Soon attain a view behind you, up-valley, northwest to Mt. Brewster and Elk Pass.

Proceed into the alpine zone on chunky talus. The slope is strewn with cairns left by idiots. Ignore them. Just keep ascending: left, near the amphitheatre edge.

This broad, rocky slope gradually narrows to a **crest** above. Pick up a bootbeaten path on the right side of the crest. Follow it. From here on, the cairns are helpful. Keep oriented by occasionally looking ahead and noting where the path climbs the mountain.

At 2546 m (8350 ft), about an hour after leaving the amphitheatre mouth, reach a seemingly vertical drop. Look closer. It's possible to carefully step down this **steep drop** to easier terrain 30 m (98 ft) below.

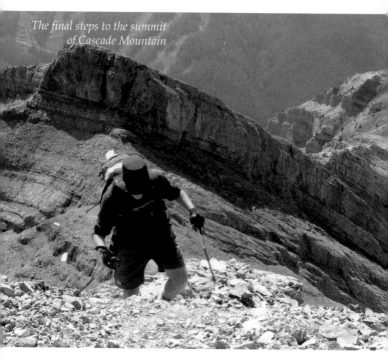

The final steps to the summit of Cascade Mountain

Beyond, the route is visible continuing east up the crest (see photo page 40) then traversing right (south). Follow the **traverse**. Above it is a false summit—a deceptive energy waster.

After rounding a **shoulder**, the route turns north-northeast. The true summit is now in view. The way forward is airy— seemingly exposed—but poses no danger if you're aware and step deliberately.

Cross a **saddle** at 2770 m (9088 ft), then begin the final steep pitch northeast. Step onto the 2997-m (9833-ft) summit of **Cascade Mtn** at 10.5 km (6.5 mi).

The panorama reveals much of southern Banff Park. South, below you, is Banff townsite. Mount Rundle is south-southeast. The Fairholme Range is east. Northeast you can see about 9 km (5.6 mi) up Lake Minnewanka.

PREPARE FOR YOUR HIKE

Hiking in the Canadian Rockies is an adventure. Adventure involves risk. But the rewards are worth it. Just be ready for more adventure than you expect.

The weather here is constantly changing. Even on a warm, sunny day, pack for rain or snow. Injury is always a possibility. On a long dayhike, be equipped to spend the night out.

If you respect the power of wilderness by being prepared, you'll decrease the risk, increase your comfort and enjoyment, and come away fulfilled, yearning for more.

You Carry What You Are

Even with all the right gear, you're ill-equipped without physical fitness.

If the weather turns grim, the physical capability to escape the wilderness fast might keep you from being stuck in a life-threatening situation. If you're fit, and a companion gets injured, you can race for help.

Besides, if you're not overweight or easily exhausted, you'll have more fun. You'll be able to hike farther, reach more spectacular scenery, and leave crowds behind.

So if you're out of shape, work on it. Everything else you'll need is easier to acquire.

Travel Light

Weight is critical when hiking, especially when backpacking. But even when dayhiking, the lighter you travel, the easier and more pleasant the journey.

Some people are mules; they can shoulder everything they might conceivably want. If you'd rather be a thoroughbred, reduce your burden by getting lighter gear and packing it with discretion.

You might have to sacrifice a few luxuries to be more agile, fleet-footed and comfortable on the trail—your bulky fleece jacket, for example, or an apple each for your spouse and three kids—but you'll be a happier hiker.

Lighter boots, clothing and packs are more expensive because the materials are finer, the engineering smarter, and the craftsmanship superior. But they're worth it. Consult reputable outdoor stores for specific brands.

Layer with Synthetics

Don't just wear a T-shirt and throw a heavy sweatshirt in your pack. Cotton kills. It quickly gets saturated with perspiration and takes way too long to dry. Wet clothing saps your body heat and could lead to hypothermia, a leading cause of death in the outdoors.

Your mountain clothes should be made of fabrics that wick sweat away from your skin, insulate when wet, and dry rapidly. Merino superfine wool, or synthetics like Capilene are ideal. Even your hiking shorts and underwear should be at least partly synthetic. Sports bras should be entirely synthetic.

Snow is possible even in summer.

There are now lots of alternatives to the soggy T-shirt. All outdoor clothing companies offer shortsleeve shirts in superior, synthetic versions. Unlike cotton T-shirts, sweat-soaked synthetics can dry during a rest break.

For warmth, several synthetic layers are more efficient than a single parka. Your body temperature varies constantly on the trail, in response to the weather and your activity level. With only one warm garment, it's either on or off, roast or freeze. Layers allow you to fine tune for optimal comfort.

In addition to a synthetic shortsleeve shirt, it's smart to pack two longsleeve tops (zip-T's) of different fabric weights: one thin, one thick. Wear the thin one for cool-weather hiking. It'll be damp when you stop for a break, so change into the thick one. When you start again, put the thin one back on.

The idea is to always keep your thick top dry in case you really need it to stay warm. Covered by a rain shell (jacket), these two tops can provide enough warmth on summer dayhikes. You can always wear your shortsleeve shirt like a vest over a longsleeve top.

For more warmth while hiking, try a fleece vest. For more warmth at rest stops, consider a down vest or down sweater. But don't hike in down clothing; it'll get sweat soaked and become useless.

For your legs, bring a pair of tights or long underwear. Choose tights made of synthetic insulating material, with a small percentage of lycra for stretch mobility. These are warmer and more durable than the all-lycra or nylon/lycra tights runners wear.

Tights are generally more efficient than pants. They stretch, conforming to your movement. They're lighter and insulate better. You can wear them for hours in a drizzle and not feel damp.

If you're too modest to sport this sleek look, bring ultralight long underwear you can slip on beneath light hiking pants—a combination that's also more wind resistant than tights.

Anticipating hot weather? Bugs? Intense sun? You'll want long pants and a longsleeve shirt, both made of tightly-woven synthetics and as lightweight as possible.

Though resembling a dress shirt or blouse—collar, button front, cuffs—your hiking shirt should be designed specifically for vigourous activity. Most outdoor clothing manufacturers offer them.

Your hiking pants should have a loose, unrestrictive fit. You can lift a knee above your hips without pulling the waistband down your butt? Perfect.

Raingear

Pack a full set of raingear: shell and pants. The shell (jacket) should have a hood. Fabrics that are both waterproof and breathable are best, because they repel rain *and* vent perspiration vapour. Gore-tex has long been the fabric of choice, but there are now many alternatives—some equally effective, others less.

Don't let a blue sky or promising weather forecast tempt you to leave your raingear behind. It can be invaluable, even if you don't encounter rain. Worn over insulating layers, a shell and pants will shed wind, retain body heat, and keep you much warmer.

Coated-nylon raingear appears to be a bargain solution, but it doesn't breathe, so it simulates a steam bath if worn while exercising. You'll end up as damp from sweat as you would from rain.

The right mountain clothing will enhance your comfort, performance and safety.

Lacking technical raingear, you're better off with a poncho. On a blustery day, a poncho won't provide impervious protection from rain, but it allows enough air circulation so you won't get sweat soaked.

Boots and Socks

Lightweight fabric boots with even a little ankle support are more stable and safer than runners. But all-leather or highly technical leather/fabric boots offer superior comfort and performance. For serious hiking, they're a necessity.

If it's a rugged, quality boot, a light- or medium-weight pair should be adequate for most hiking conditions. Heavy boots will slow you down, just like an overweight pack. But you want boots with hard, protective toes, or you'll risk a broken or sprained digit.

Lateral support stops ankle injuries. Stiff shanks keep your feet from tiring. Grippy outsoles prevent slipping and falling. And sufficient cushioning lessens the pain of a long day on the trail.

Out of the box, boots should be waterproof or at least very water resistant, although you'll have to treat them often to maintain their repellency. Boots with lots of seams allow water to seep in as they age. A full rand (wraparound bumper) adds an extra measure of water protection.

The key consideration is comfort. Make sure your boots don't hurt. If you wait to find out until after a day of hiking, it's too late; you're stuck with them. So before purchasing, ask the retailer if, after wearing them indoors, you can exchange them if they don't feel right. A half-hour of walking in a hotel or mall is a helpful test.

Socks are important too. To keep your feet dry, warm and happy, wear wool, thick acrylic, or wool/acrylic-blend socks. Cotton socks retain sweat, cause blisters, and are especially bad if your boots aren't waterproof. It's usually best to wear two pairs of socks, with a thinner, synthetic pair next to your feet to wick away moisture and alleviate friction, minimizing the chance of blisters.

Gloves and Hats

Always bring gloves and a hat. You've probably heard it, and it's true: your body loses most of its heat through your head and extremities. Cover them if you get chilled. Carry thin, synthetic gloves to wear while hiking. Don't worry if they get wet, but keep a pair of thicker fleece gloves dry in your pack. A fleece hat, or at least a thick headband that covers your ears, adds a lot of warmth and weighs little. A hat with a long brim is essential to shade your eyes and protect your face from sun exposure.

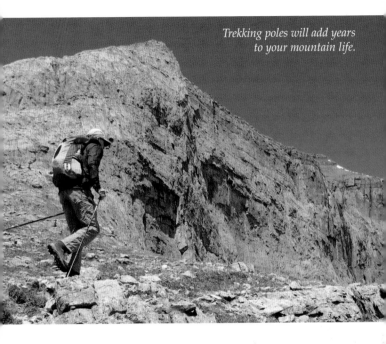

Trekking poles will add years to your mountain life.

Trekking Poles

Long, steep ascents and descents in the Canadian Rockies make trekking poles vital. Hiking with poles is easier, more enjoyable, and less punishing to your body. If you're constantly pounding the trails, they could add years to your mountain life.

Working on a previous guidebook, we once hiked for a month without poles. Both of us developed knee pain. The next summer we used Leki trekking poles every day for three months and our knees were never strained. We felt like four-legged animals. We were more surefooted. Our speed and endurance increased.

Studies show that during a typical eight-hour hike you'll transfer more than 250 tons of pressure to a pair of trekking poles. When going downhill, poles significantly reduce stress to your knees, as well as your ankles and lower back.

They alleviate knee strain when you're going uphill too, because you're climbing with your arms and shoulders, not just your legs. Poles also improve your posture. They keep you more upright, which gives you greater lung capacity and allows more efficient breathing.

Regardless how light your daypack is, you'll appreciate the support of trekking poles. They're especially helpful for crossing unbridged streams, traversing steep slopes, and negotiating muddy, rooty, rough stretches of trail.

Poles prevent ankle sprains—a common hiking injury. By making you more stable, they actually help you relax, boosting your sense of security and confidence.

Don't carry one of those big, heavy, gnarled, wooden staffs, unless you're going to a costume party dressed as Gandalf. They're more burden than benefit.

A pair of old ski poles will suffice. They're not as effective or comfortable as poles designed specifically for trekking, but they're better than hiking empty handed.

If possible, invest in a pair of true trekking poles with a soft anti-shock system and adjustable, telescoping, super-lock shafts. We strongly recommend Lekis.

First Aid

Someone in your hiking party should carry a first-aid kit. Prepackaged kits look handy, but they're expensive, and some are inadequate. If you make your own, you'll be more familiar with the contents.

Include an antibacterial ointment; pain pills with ibuprofen, and a few with codeine for agonizing injuries; regular bandages; several sizes of butterfly bandages; a couple bandages big enough to hold a serious laceration together; rolls of sterile gauze and absorbent pads to staunch bleeding; adhesive tape; tiny fold-up scissors or a small knife; and a compact first-aid manual.

Whether your kit is store bought or homemade, check the expiration dates on your medications every year and replace them as needed.

Instead of the old elastic bandages for wrapping sprains, we now carry neoprene ankle and knee bands. They slip on instantly, require no special wrapping technique, keep the injured joint warmer, and stay in place better. They're so convenient, you can quickly slip them on for extra support on long, steep, rough descents.

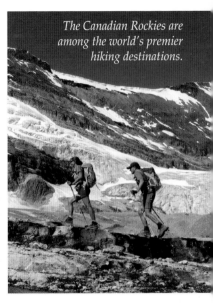

The Canadian Rockies are among the world's premier hiking destinations.

Bandanas

A bandana will be the most versatile item in your pack. Carry at least two when dayhiking.

You can use a bandana to blow your nose, mop your brow, or improvise a beanie. It makes a colourful headband that will keep sweat or hair out of your eyes. It serves as a bandage or sling in a medical emergency.

Worn as a neckerchief, a bandana prevents a sunburned neck. If you soak it in water, then drape it around your neck, it will help keep you from overheating.

Worn Lawrence-of-Arabia style under a hat, a bandana shades both sides of your face, as well as your neck, while deterring mosquitoes. For an air-conditioning effect, soak it in water then don it á la Lawrence.

When shooing away bugs, flicking a bandana with your wrist is less tiresome than flailing your arms.

Small and Essential

A closed-cell foam pad, just big enough to sit on, weighs little but makes rest breaks more comfortable and therefore restful. If an emergency ever forces you to spend a night out, having a foam pad might be the difference between a tolerable experience and a miserable one.

In a crisis, it might be necessary to start a fire to keep warm. Carry matches in a plastic bag, so they'll stay dry. It's wise to have a lighter, too. Finger-size fire starters (Optimus Firelighter or Coghlan FireSticks) are a godsend in wet weather.

Pack an emergency survival bag. One fits into the palm of your hand and could help you survive a cold night without a sleeping bag or tent. The ultralight, metallic fabric reflects your body heat back at you. Survival bags, which you crawl into, are more efficient than survival blankets.

Bring plastic bags in various sizes. Use the small ones for packing whatever garbage you generate or find. A couple large trash bags could be used to improvise a shelter.

A headlamp is often helpful and can be necessary for safety. You'll need one to stay on the trail if you're forced to hike after sunset. Carry spare batteries.

Most people find mosquito repellent indispensable. If you anticipate an infestation, bring a head net made of fine, nylon mesh.

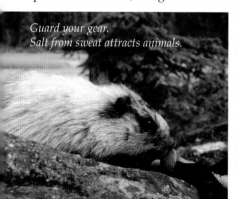

Guard your gear.
Salt from sweat attracts animals.

For those dreaded blisters, pack Moleskin or Spenco gel. Cut it with the knife or scissors you should have in your first-aid kit.

Wind and glare will quickly strain your eyes and might give you a headache. Sun exposure can cause cataracts and cancer. Wear sunglasses, a hat with a brim, and sunscreen.

Remember to stuff your brain with provocative questions to ask your companions. Hiking stimulates meaningful conversation.

Keep It All Dry

Most packs are not waterproof, or even very water resistant. To protect your gear from rain, put it in plastic bags and use a waterproof pack cover. Rain is a constant likelihood, so you might as well start hiking with everything in bags. That's easier than wrestling with it in a storm. For added assurance, light-weight, waterproof stuffsacks are superior to plastic bags.

Water

Drink water frequently. Keeping your body hydrated is essential. If you're thirsty, you're probably not performing at optimal efficiency.

But be aware of giardia lamblia, a waterborne parasitic cyst that causes severe gastrointestinal distress. It's transported through animal and human feces, so never defecate or urinate near water.

To be safe, assume giardia is present in all surface water in the Canadian Rockies. Don't drink any water unless it's directly from a source you're certain is pure, like meltwater dripping off glacial ice, or until you've disinfected or filtered it.

Killing giardia by disinfecting it with iodine tablets can be tricky. The colder the water, the longer you must wait. Iodine also makes the water smell and taste awful, unless you use neutralizing pills. And iodine has no effect whatsoever on cryptosporidium, an increasingly common cyst that causes physical symptoms identical to giardiasis.

Carrying a small, lightweight filter is a reasonable solution. Some filters weigh just 240 grams (8 ounces). To strain out giardia cysts, your filter must have an absolute pore size of 4 microns or less. Straining out cryptosporidium cysts requires an absolute pore size of 2 microns or less.

After relying on water filters for many years, we've switched to Pristine water purification droplets (www.pristine.ca). The active ingredient is chlorine dioxide, which has been used for more than 50 years in hundreds of water treatment plants throughout North America and Europe.

The Pristine system comprises two 30-ml bottles with a total combined weight of only 80 grams (2.8 ounces). It purifies up to 120 litres (30 gallons) of water. Using it is simple: mix two solutions, wait five minutes, then add it to your water. You can drink 15 minutes later knowing you won't contract giardia. Treating for cryptosporidium requires a higher dosage and/or longer wait.

Body Fuel

When planning meals, keep energy and nutrition foremost in mind. During a six-hour hike, you'll burn 1800 to 3000 calories, depending on terrain, pace, body size, and pack weight. You'll be stronger, and therefore safer and happier, if you tank up on high-octane body fuel.

A white-flour bun with a thick slab of meat or cheese on it is low-octane fuel. Too much protein or fat will make you feel sluggish and drag you down. And you won't get very far up the trail snacking on candy bars. Refined sugars give you a brief spurt that quickly fizzles.

For sustained exercise, like hiking, you need protein and fat to function normally and give you that satisfying full feeling. The speed of your metabolism determines how much protein and fat you should eat. Both are hard to digest. Your body takes three or four hours to assimilate them, compared to one or two hours for carbohydrates.

That's why a carb-heavy diet is optimal for hiking. It ensures your blood supply keeps hustling oxygen to your legs, instead of diverted it to your stomach. Most people, however, can sustain athletic effort longer if their carb-heavy diet includes a little protein. So eat a small portion of protein in the morning, a smaller portion at lunch, and a moderate portion at dinner to aid muscle repair.

For athletic performance, the American and Canadian Dietetic Association recommends that 60 to 65% of your total energy come from carbs, less than 25% from fat, and 15% from protein. They also say refined carbs and sugars should account for no more than 10% of your total carb calories.

Toiling muscles crave the glycogen your body manufactures from complex carbs. Yet your body has limited carb storage capacity. So your carb intake should be constant. That means loading your pack with plant foods made of whole-grain flour, rice, corn, oats, legumes, nuts, seeds, fruit and vegetables.

Dining Out

Natural- or health-food stores are reliable sources of hiking food. They even stock energy bars, which are superior to candy bars because they contain more carbs and less fat.

Always bring a few more energy bars than you think you'll need. Our favourites are made by Honey Stinger, Clif Bar, and PowerBar. They energize us faster and sustain us longer than others we've tried.

For lunch, how about a whole-grain pita pocket filled with tabouli, hummus, avocado, cucumbers and sprouts?

Another favourite of ours is marinated tofu that's been pressed, baked, and vacuum-packed. It's protein rich, delicious, and lasts unrefrigerated for more than a day.

Omnivores have other excellent protein options: hard-boiled eggs, free-range bison jerky, and vacuum-packed wild salmon in tear-open bags. Eat cheese sparingly; beyond small amounts, it's unhealthy.

In addition to our main course, we usually bring a bag of organic tortilla chips (corn or mixed-grain) cooked in expeller-pressed safflower or canola oil.

For snacks, carry dried fruit; whole-grain cookies made with natural sweeteners (brown-rice syrup, organic cane-sugar, fruit juice, raw honey); or whole-grain crackers.

Steep terrain like Cory Pass demands high-octane body fuel.

INDEX

INFORMATION SOURCES

Banff National Park
www.pc.gc.ca/banff

Banff Tourism
www.banfflakelouise.com

Weather
www.theweathernetwork.com

Mountain goat

THE AUTHORS

Kathy and Craig are dedicated to each other, and to hiking, in that order. Their second date was a 32-km (20-mile) dayhike in Arizona. Since then they haven't stopped for long.

They've trekked through much of the world's vertical topography, including the Himalayas, Patagonian Andes, Spanish Pyrenees, Swiss Alps, Scottish Highlands, Italian Dolomites, and New Zealand Alps. In North America, they've explored the B.C. Coast, Selkirk and Purcell ranges, Montana's Beartooth Wilderness, Wyoming's Grand Tetons, the California Sierra, Washington's North Cascades, and the Colorado Rockies.

In 1989 they moved from the U.S. to Canada, so they could live near the Canadian Rockies—the range that inspired the first of their refreshingly unconventional guidebooks: *Don't Waste*

Your Time in the Canadian Rockies, The Opinionated Hiking Guide. Its popularity encouraged them to abandon their careers—Kathy as an ESL teacher, Craig as an ad-agency creative director—and start their own guidebook publishing company: hikingcamping.com.

Though the distances they hike are epic, Kathy and Craig agree that hiking, no matter how far, is the easiest of the many tasks necessary to create a guidebook. What they find most challenging is having to sit at their Canmore, Alberta, home, with the Canadian Rockies visible out the window. But they do it every winter, spending twice as much time at their computers—writing, organizing, editing, checking facts—as they do on the trail.

The result is worth it. Kathy and Craig's colourful writing, opinionated commentary, and enthusiasm for the joys of hiking make their guidebooks uniquely helpful and compelling.

Other Titles from hikingcamping.com

The following titles—boot-tested and written by the Opinionated Hikers, Kathy & Craig Copeland—are widely available at outdoor shops and bookstores. Visit www.hikingcamping.com to read excerpts and purchase online. The website is also where Kathy and Craig frequently blog about hiking and camping worldwide. Each post emphasizes practical advice you can use when planning your next hiking or camping trip.

Don't Waste Your Time in the Canadian Rockies®
The Opinionated Hiking Guide

ISBN 978-0978342753 Even here, in a mountain range designated a UNESCO World Heritage Site for its "superlative natural phenomena" and "exceptional natural beauty and aesthetic importance," not all scenery is equal. Some destinations are simply more striking, more intriguing, more inspiring than others. Now you can be certain you're choosing a rewarding hike for your weekend or vacation. This uniquely helpful, visually captivating guidebook covers Banff, Jasper, Kootenay, Yoho and Waterton Lakes national parks, plus Mt. Robson and Mt. Assiniboine provincial parks. It rates each trail *Premier, Outstanding, Worthwhile,* or *Don't Do*, explains why, and provides comprehensive route descriptions. 138 dayhikes and backpack trips. Trail maps for each hike. 544 pages, 270 photos, full colour throughout. 6th edition January 2011.

Where Locals Hike
in the Canadian Rockies
The Premier Trails in Kananaskis
Country, near Canmore and Calgary

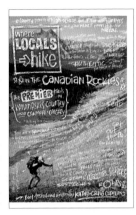

ISBN 978-0-9783427-4-6 The 55 most rewarding dayhikes and backpack trips within two hours of Calgary's international airport. All lead to astonishing alpine meadows, ridges and peaks. Though these trails are little known compared to those in the nearby Canadian Rocky Mountain national parks, the scenery is equally magnificent. Includes Peter Lougheed and Spray Valley provincial parks. Discerning trail reviews help you choose your trip. Detailed route descriptions keep you on the path. 320 pages, 180 photos, trail maps for each hike, full colour throughout. 3rd edition May 2012.

Where Locals Hike
in the West Kootenay
The Premier Trails in Southeast B.C.
near Kaslo & Nelson

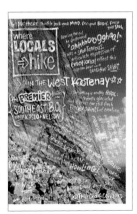

ISBN 978-0-9689419-9-7 See the peaks, glaciers and cascades that make locals passionate about these mountains. The 50 most rewarding dayhikes and backpack trips in the Selkirk and west Purcell ranges of southeast British Columbia. Includes Valhalla, Kokanee Glacier, and Goat Range parks, as well as hikes near Arrow, Slocan, and Kootenay lakes. Discerning trail reviews help you choose your trip. Detailed route descriptions keep you on the path. 272 pages, 130 photos, trail locator maps, full colour throughout. Updated 3rd edition Spring 2012.

Camp Free in B.C.

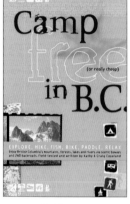

ISBN 978-0-9735099-3-9 Make your weekend or vacation adventurous and revitalizing. Enjoy British Columbia's scenic byways and 2WD backroads—in your low-clearance car or your big RV. Follow precise directions to 350 campgrounds, from the B.C. Coast to the Rocky Mountains. Choose from 80 low-fee campgrounds similar in quality to provincial parks but half the price. Find retreats where the world is yours alone. Simplify life: slow down, ease up. Fully appreciate B.C.'s magnificent backcountry, including the Sunshine Coast, Okanagan, Shuswap Highlands, Selkirk and Purcell ranges, Cariboo Mountains, and Chilcotin Plateau. 544 pages, 200 photos, 20 regional maps, full colour throughout. Updated 4th edition June 2011.

Gotta Camp Alberta

ISBN 978-0-9735099-0-8 Make your weekend or vacation adventurous and revitalizing. Enjoy Alberta's scenic byways and 2WD backroads—in your low-clearance car or your big RV. Follow precise directions to 150 idyllic campgrounds, from the foothill lakes to the Rocky Mountains. Camp in national parks, provincial parks, and recreation areas. Find retreats where the world is yours alone. Simplify life: slow down, ease up. Return home soothed by the serenity of nature. Approximately 400 pages, 170 photos, and 18 maps. Full colour throughout. First edition June 2012.

Heading Outdoors Eventually Leads Within
Thoughts Inspired by
30,000 Miles on the Trail

ISBN 978-0-9783427-6-0 Everyone walks. What distinguishes hikers is that walking does more than transport us, it transforms us. But nowhere is the thoughtful undercurrent of hiking celebrated. The wisdom we glean from the wilds is a match lit in the rain. That's why we created this book: to cup our hands around the flame. These journal entries are the mental waypoints we recorded while hiking 30,000 miles (more than the circumference of the Earth) through wildlands worldwide. Accompanying them are photos of the places (primarily the Canadian Rockies, Utah canyon country, and New Zealand) where we conceived and noted the initial ideas. A truly adventurous life is contemplative as well as vigourous. Hardcover, 96 pages, 72 full-colour photos. First edition January 2011.

Hiking from Here to WOW: Utah Canyon Country
95 Trails to the Wonder of Wilderness

ISBN 978-0-89997-452-1 The authors hiked more than 1,600 miles through Zion, Bryce, Escalante-Grand Staircase, Glen Canyon, Grand Gulch, Cedar Mesa, Canyonlands, Moab, Arches, Capitol Reef, and the San Rafael Swell. They took more than 2,500 photos and hundreds of pages of field notes. Then they culled their list of favourite hikes down to 95 trips—each selected for its power to incite awe. Their 480-page book describes where to find the redrock cliffs, slickrock domes, soaring arches, and ancient ruins that make southern Utah unique in all the world. And it does so in refreshing style: honest, literate, entertaining, inspiring. Like all *WOW Guides*, this one is full colour throughout, with 220 photos and a trail map for each dayhike and backpack trip. Updated 1ˢᵗ edition November 2010.

Done in a Day: Jasper
The 10 Premier Hikes

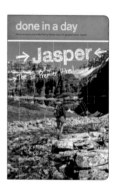

ISBN 978-0-9783427-1-5 Where to invest your limited hiking time to enjoy the greatest scenic reward. Choose an easy, vigourous, or challenging hike. Start your adventure within a short drive of town. Witness the wonder of Jasper National Park and be back for a hot shower, great meal, and soft bed. 128 pages, 75 photos, trail maps for each trip, full colour throughout. Updated first edition June 2011.

Done in a Day: Whistler
The 10 Premier Hikes

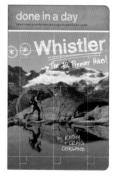

ISBN 978-0-9735099-7-7 Where to invest your limited hiking time to enjoy the greatest scenic reward. Choose an easy, vigourous, or challenging hike. Start your adventure within a short drive of the village. Witness the wonder of Whistler, British Columbia, and be back for a hot shower, great meal, and soft bed. 144 pages, 80 photos, trail maps for each trip, full colour throughout. First edition December 2007.

Done in a Day: Moab
The 10 Premier Hikes

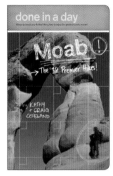

ISBN 978-0-9735099-8-4 Where to invest your limited hiking time to enjoy the greatest scenic reward. Choose an easy, vigourous, or challenging hike. Start your adventure within a short drive of town. Witness the wonder of canyon country—including Arches and Canyonlands national parks—and be back for a hot shower, great meal, and soft bed. 160 pages, 110 photos, trail maps for each trip, full colour throughout. First edition February 2008.

Done in a Day: Calgary
The 10 Premier Road Rides

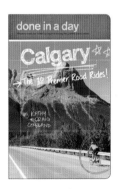

ISBN 978-0-9783427-3-9 Where to invest your limited cycling time to enjoy the greatest scenic reward. Spring through fall, southwest Alberta offers cyclists blue-ribbon road riding: from alpine passes in the Canadian Rockies, to dinosaur-country river canyons on the edge of the prairie. And this compact, jersey-pocket-sized book is your guide to the crème de la crème: the ten most serene, compelling, bike-friendly roads in the region. Start pedaling within a short drive of Calgary. At day's end, be back for a hot shower, great meal, and soft bed. 120 pages, 80 photos, road maps for each ride, full colour throughout. First edition December 2007.

Bears Beware!
Warning Calls You Can Make
to Avoid an Encounter

Here's the 30-minute MP3 that could save your life. Download it from hikingcamping.com to your computer. Go to Guidebooks > Hiking > Canadian Rockies. Listen to it at home, or on your iPod while driving to the trailhead.

You'll find out why pepper spray, talking, and bells are insufficient protection. You'll realize that using your voice is the only reliable method of preventing a bear encounter. You'll discover why warning calls are the key to defensive hiking. You'll understand how, where and when to make warning calls. You'll learn specific strategies for worry-free hiking and camping in bear country.

Bears Beware! was endorsed by the wardens at Jasper National Park, which has the biggest grizzly-bear population in the Canadian Rockies. It was also approved by the wardens at Waterton National Park, which has the highest concentration of grizzly bears in the Rockies.

Mt. Fifi, from Cory Pass (Trip 7)